FROM IDEA TO WEB STARTUP

in 21 *Days*

Creating bacn.com

JASON GLASPEY WITH **SCOTT KVETON**

Peachpit
Press

FROM IDEA TO WEB STARTUP IN 21 DAYS: CREATING BACN.COM
Jason Glaspey with Scott Kveton

New Riders
1249 Eighth Street
Berkeley, CA 94710
510/524-2178
510/524-2221 (fax)
Find us on the Web at www.newriders.com
To report errors, please send a note to errata@peachpit.com
New Riders is an imprint of Peachpit, a division of Pearson Education

Editor: WENDY SHARP
Production Coordinator: MYRNA VLADIC
Copyeditor: WENDY KATZ
Compositor: DAVID VAN NESS
Indexer: VALERIE HAYNES PERRY
Cover design: MIMI HEFT
Interior design: CHRIS GILLESPIE, HAPPENSTANCE TYPE-O-RAMA

ISBN 13: 978-0-321-71428-2
ISBN 10:   0-321-71428-8

9 8 7 6 5 4 3 2 1

Printed and bound in the United States of America

FROM MICHAEL

To Susan for encouraging me along, even though she's a vegetarian and hated how the house smelled, and Hayes for being willing to go along my godawful experiments in bacon exploration.

FROM SCOTT

To Kami, for packing and shipping all that bacon almost every day, with the kids in tow the whole time.

FROM JASON

To my brother-in-law who taught me the "swirl" bacon cooking technique, and to Holly, for putting up with me telling her how to design things.

CONTENTS

SELLING BACON?

WHEN PEOPLE ASK us what we do, we tell them we sell bacon on the Internet. There's usually a moment of confusion, followed by semi-understanding.

"Wait. What? What do you mean, you sell bacon online. Like, real bacon?"

"Yeah. We sell packages of bacon."

"Like real bacon, you sell it online?"

"Yeah."

"Cool." Followed by a pause while they consider the facts.

"So, you just take orders, right? You don't ship it or anything, do you?"

"Actually, we do. We have a fridge in our office—it's stuffed full of bacon right now. We get it from all over the country, but mostly from small farms with happy pigs."

"Wow… That's awesome."

It's also only partially true. The three of us—your authors, Jason Glaspey and Scott Kveton, and our associate, Michael Richardson—are the founders of Bac'n, an online bacon retailer located at bacn.com. It was a business started in three weeks, built in our spare time, and operated as a side project.

Side project or not, it was an experience we learned a lot from, and one that others can learn from, too. With agile web development and agile business practices, almost anyone can start a business in a matter of days. While once you might have spent months refining your business goals and writing business plans, researching, talking to investors and banks, and getting loans, today you can almost launch on an idea and figure it out as you go. Money is no longer the barrier it used to be, and neither is time.

You truly can start a fully-functioning, this-is-really-a-business company, all while keeping it a side project and working full time at a "normal" job.

WHY A BOOK?

In the beginning, it was a simple idea—start a business around bacon and sell it online. But our approach to "launch first and ask questions later" resonates with people, and we're often asked about it.

Did we do everything right? No. But we did many things good enough (our editor begged to change this to "well enough" but this is OUR book!), and in the modern business world, good enough in practice is often better than perfect in theory.

We wrote this book to help you follow along our path, the lessons we learned, the software we used, our mistakes, and our good fortune. Sometimes, though, we'll just tell our story. We hope you'll learn from our experiences, avoid our mistakes, and be inspired by our results. And we hope it will help you start your own project, and that—as we did—you'll have a great time doing it, create a business you're proud of, and maybe even make some money.

WHY 21 DAYS?

From the beginning, all three of us were committed to doing Bac'n using the approach of agile software development. The process focuses on launching fast and early, and adjusting on the fly. Agile software development is arguably most famous as the way in which 37signals works; they've built an impressive lineup of wildly successful online business software all without ever taking funding and keeping their staff at a bare minimum. Their most popular tool is Basecamp, which, appropriately enough, we used to manage our project, Bac'n.

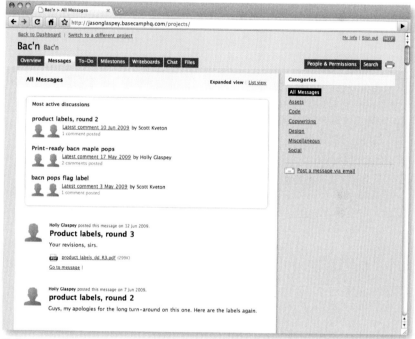

■ Basecamp is where we managed all of our files, messages, and to-dos.

Looking back, our three-week deadline probably saved the project. If we hadn't had that timeline, we would have spent three months or more creating the site. It would have dragged on and on, and we would've worked on it much too slowly. Our artificial restriction kept us moving, gave us clarity, and required that we didn't spend countless hours debating one way to do something over another.

We've since worked on a few other projects and startups, and have passionately advocated this same method. Bac'n might not have come into existence had we spent three months building it, and if it had, it's doubtful it would have been a single ounce better.

Until we had real customers, we could only guess what they really wanted. But on the web, we could add, edit, or change both the content and the business plan as we went along. We were able to adapt as necessary to better meet our customers' needs—right as we recognized them.

Remember, the web is never finished.

You'll never launch a site and be done with it, so don't worry too much about getting everything right the first time. There's always a chance to correct a path, but you have to be in motion to do so. Hopefully, this book helps you put aside your fears and get into motion.

chapter 1

WHY BACON?

PEOPLE LOVE BACON. It's hard to say why, but people just seem to have a passion about this particular food item that you don't find with other things, even other types of pork. And while people have probably always loved bacon, it seems to be around mid-2007 that bacon started moving into the category of "meme."

At first, it was kind of a publicly-known inside joke: pronouncing your love for bacon defiant of the general knowledge that bacon was unhealthy. And any bacon-related products, be it band-aids or T-shirts, would win you little comments of adoration when you wore them or set them on your desk at the office.

meme (noun)

1. an idea, belief or belief system, or pattern of behavior that spreads throughout a culture either vertically by cultural inheritance (as by parents to children) or horizontally by cultural acquisition (as by peers, information media, and entertainment media)

2. a pervasive thought or thought pattern that replicates itself via cultural means; a parasitic code, a virus of the mind especially contagious to children and the impressionable

3. the fundamental unit of information, analogous to the gene in emerging evolutionary theory of culture

4. in blogspeak, an idea that is spread from blog to blog

5. an Internet information generator, especially of random or contentless information

(Etymology : meme : derived from the Greek mimēma, 'something imitated,' by Richard Dawkins in 1976)

www.urbandictionary.com

At the time, Jason was working at an interactive agency with his good friend, developer Matt King. Matt had recently started a blog called thebacondesk.com, showcasing the novel, bacon-related products that were popping up all over. Jason helped with posting new content when he could, and they frequently joked between them about who loved bacon more.

One afternoon Matt sent Jason a link via instant message, glanced over and said, "This should be arriving sometime today."

As Jason clicked the link he saw the first proof that bacon was tipping. It was BaconSalt®—a condiment in a shaker that makes everything you apply it to taste like bacon.

■ A nice little family pack of BaconSalt and Baconnaise

When it came later that day, everyone in the office gathered around and poured it on everything they could find (popcorn being the most highly anticipated test-case). There was something perfect about it: it was both a ridiculous novelty item and a pretty decent condiment. Everyone laughed at it—and fought over it at the same time.

Yes, bacon was becoming a meme, and the Internet only gave it wings. Every week another product—bacon mints, bacon band-aids, bacon-covered doughnuts, bacon bras—hit the Internets. And we—Scott and Jason—were chronicling it all.

■ Bacon-topped Maple Bars from Voodoo Doughnuts in Portland, Oregon

Two sites, bacongeek.com and thebacondesk.com, were blogging about the spectacle. Scott wrote for BaconGeek, Matt and Jason for thebacondesk.com. Was this really the path to starting our own company? Turns out, it was.

THE TEAM

In November of 2008, the three of us might have seemed like unlikely partners in a startup. Jason was in South America, and Scott and Michael were working at Vidoop, a startup in its own right. But we were drawn together by our love for bacon, solidified by our unique capabilities, and ignited by our excitement for making something that was our own.

We fell into three critical roles: the deal-maker, the promoter, and the builder.

SCOTT KVETON, THE DEAL-MAKER

Scott was getting restless. Vidoop was a big company with big ideas, which made results and change slow to happen. To Scott, the idea of starting his own company was enticing. Working quick and agile, running lean with just a few people working hard, and keeping overhead near zero was the business style he really wanted to be working in. Also, going from secure logins for identity to actually shipping a tangible product was a very different beast to tackle.

Scott was a technologist by trade, having worked at large companies (Amazon.com) and run smaller ones (JanRain). He was also very active in the burgeoning open-source software scene and open web standards groups. He was no stranger to taking a few risks and trying something new.

But outside of his day job in technology, he'd always been known for foody inclinations and his semi-yearly pizza parties. He'd invite over a swarm of people and make homemade pizza all day long. He was always cooking different things, and was regularly finding his culinary efforts centering on bacon. He started his own blog capturing both the crazy things people were doing with bacon online, but also his own pursuits, from making his own bacon from pork bellies to BBQing bacon and putting photos and video online to document the process.

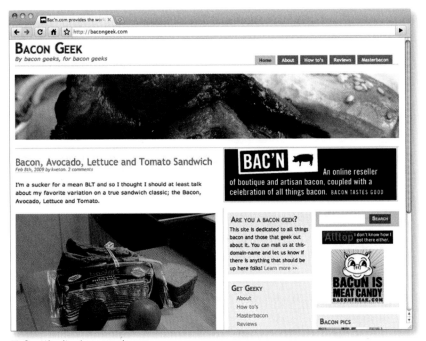

■ Scott's site, bacongeek.com

And as Scott was discovering, he was not only becoming known for bacon—bacon was becoming more than a novelty or a joke. Bacon had some weird quality that brought people together: everyone loved eating it, and everyone loved talking about it. It also was something kind of cool. When you talked about it, you felt cool as well.

With this rise in geek chic also came a rise in business opportunities, and lots of people were cashing in. The problem was, most of it wasn't practical or something you'd buy twice. There were lots of products, but few real businesses.

While Scott continued to cook, blog, tweet, and photograph bacon, his own identity online started to reflect it, and he started looking for a way to cash in for himself.

JASON GLASPEY, THE PROMOTER

Jason Glaspey had worked on a handful of side projects through his early career, a few of them modestly successful. He'd built a happy-hour finder called Unthirsty.com with partner and former co-worker, Matt King, where you could map and plot your wanderings in search of cheap eats, and he'd finagled an opportunity to review cars for a few years after leaving his position at the website for a car magazine.

He was always looking for something fun, profitable, and where he could learn. He wasn't a programmer or a designer, but he had a good instinct towards business ideas and making those millions of tiny decisions that every project faces. He also had an advertising background, and so was familiar with brand and strategy and marketing.

Jason had been an interactive producer at a web development agency until he wandered off to South America for a few months. But his time working with and producing sites for global brands gave him a strong sense of the user experience and the importance of branding, and his passion for side-projects—where he usually learned his biggest lessons—kept him on the lookout for experiences along the periphery.

■ In Chile, Jason found a quaint restaurant that brought out an entire grill filled with meat right to our table. This photo is what was left after we ate most of it.

In working on Bac'n, he got to stretch his skills, work with people he respected in the local community, and be around one of his favorite food items of all time. Plus, what's cooler than selling bacon online?

■ MICHAEL RICHARDSON, THE DEVELOPER

Michael was a young and ambitiously busy programmer looking for more ways to practice his trade. Like many developers, learning new things and being stretched was a big part of job satisfaction for him. After starting his career doing technology for a political consulting company, he realized that full-time development was where he belonged. Creating projects, tools, and utilities was a dream. He quickly got involved in Portland's local tech scene, learning as much as he could and trying to contribute back where possible. As one of those kids who was always selling lemonade growing up, he gravitated to the startup scene, where the rampant entrepreneurism suited him perfectly.

Michael had his own path to bacon. Cooking had always been a favorite pastime of his, and focusing on fine food was a passion. He also firmly believed that the best meals start with the best ingredients. Getting to eat and work on a project centered around finding the best bacon from the country's best farms was right up his alley. More importantly, the challenge to rapidly create and ship a full business was very appealing.

FREE BACON: A GOOD REASON TO BE IN THE BUSINESS

Scott started reaching out to different farms and places that sold bacon online. He wanted to get a feel for the different bacons out there, and see if there was a difference between what we got here on the west coast and what was available elsewhere in the country. He'd heard about a certain bacon brand that got rave reviews online, and ordered some to try. When it came, he was shocked.

It was terrible.

This was bacon people honestly believed was fantastic.

In that instant he had a moment of clarity: "People don't know what good bacon is." It was simple and, sadly, true.

But it turned out to be a great discovery. It told him that if he could get high-quality bacon to people, they'd come back for more—and they'd tell their friends. And judging by the way people were already raving about this bad bacon, there was a huge opportunity to be filled. He noticed the volume of people talking about this bacon, how much they were paying for it, and how little they were getting.

This was exactly the market to upend.

ASSEMBLING THE TEAM

Michael and Scott were good friends who worked together at Vidoop. As their conversations of this and that regularly returned to bacon, Scott clued Michael in on his idea. He was still working out the details, but the idea of being the sole developer in a business that sold bacon online was too much for Michael to resist, and he signed up immediately to be in charge of development.

Around the same time in November 2008, Scott decided that instead of another pizza party, he'd throw a bacon-themed get-together. While he was beginning to investigate this bacon business idea, the party was largely an independent concept at this point. And as word of the party got out, the list of attendees grew.

When Scott told Jason about the party, Jason made him promise he'd wait until January so Jason could attend after he got back from South America. In return, Scott made him help with the planning. It didn't take long until they decided a small and modest party wouldn't be appropriate for their course of honor, and they decided to take it over the top, to make it an epic event.

 ## Choosing Good Partners

YOU REALLY CAN'T say enough about how important it is to start out with a good group that really works well together. Don't forget, this is a business we're talking about—it's not personal. We've seen a lot of projects stall because the wrong people tried to work together. Here are some things to keep in mind when you're choosing a team:

- Do you have the same level of dedication? Are you all committed to making it work? If you're counting on someone to be completely committed to an idea, and they have three or four other things going on or are only into it because it sounded "fun," it's going to cause a lot of frustration.

- What does success mean to each of you? If one person is hoping to get acquired and cash in, and another is hoping to build a lifestyle business that'll run for 30 years, you're going to have some conflict.

- What do you know about each other's past work experiences? People who work on side projects probably have several in their repertoire. Look at how dedicated they were to those projects and talk to the people they worked with. You want to have an idea of someone's work ethic and team attitude before you get started.

Just because someone has initial excitement for an idea and the necessary ability to do the job does not mean they will be a good partner, or even the right partner for you. Someone who is flaky early on is going to be terrible later when the excitement of the project has worn off. Don't feel bad about honestly telling someone they're not right for the project.

Remember, you'll be able to change almost everything about your project later, but it's very difficult to change your team.

While Jason and Scott were chatting about the bacon party, Scott said he'd love to run some ideas by Jason about a business plan. They kept chatting, and trading thoughts while planning for the party. Within a few weeks Scott had shared enough about the project and had enjoyed the event planning enough that the two agreed to go in on the project together.

So here we were, Scott, Michael, and Jason—all excited and committed to this idea of building a business about bacon. We still didn't really understand what we were in for, nor had we really grasped what the details of this bacon business would be, but we liked the sound of it, and literally, the taste as well.

BEYOND THE BACON: BRAND DECISIONS AND GETTING DOWN TO WORK

So now we had a team in place, and the rough idea to sell bacon online. We were chatting daily about all the different details, but there wasn't really a stake in the ground, nor a specific goal to reach for. The holidays were fast approaching as well, and we knew it would be hard to get much done during December.

WHERE'S THE BACON?

In the meantime, Scott made an executive decision and purchased the domain bacn.com, as well as bacn.me. We weren't immediately sure what we'd do with bacn.me, but we had some ideas, and it was cheap. The primary domain, however, wasn't as cheap as we'd have liked. The domain's price tag included a comma—although it contained only four digits—and was by far the most expensive piece of our young startup.

We all agreed that buying a .com domain was important. It's not critical, and there have been many successful startups that have used .org and .net top-level-domains, but we felt that would be working with a small handicap and could be avoided. It's so much easier when your brand exactly mirrors your domain *and* ends in .com. When you tell someone your company name, and they go and look it up later on, it's very common for them to assume it's a .com, and we didn't want to have to constantly be working against that.

 Who Pays the Bills?

MICHAEL AND JASON liked to think Scott was making too much money at Vidoop, so neither felt too bad about him footing the bill for the domain himself. Besides, this was his idea; he was funding the company out of pocket from the beginning. Michael and Jason were working for equity. Not to overshare, but by not having much cash in the game, they both had less commitment to the cause, as well as getting a lesser share in equity. This wasn't—and isn't—really a problem, but know that just because you start something with other people, it doesn't have to be all even-steven.

■ MARKET RESEARCH AND A VISION

As part of our market research, Scott reached out to Rocco, creator of Bacon Freak. Rocco had created a successful business by saturating the bacon-internet with his T-shirt "Bacon is Meat Candy." He also white-labeled a few different types of bacon from some of the very farms we were talking to, and a few we hadn't yet connected with. In addition, he sold bacon jerky and a few novelty items on his site.

■ The "Bacon is Meat Candy" T-shirt

Scott was pretty forthcoming with him in the early stages about our plans, and Rocco was incredibly open with us in return, sharing quite a bit about his numbers, volume, and margins. We learned that he sold plenty of bacon, plenty of T-shirts, and had a large subscriber base to his monthly bacon club, which sent new bacon to your door automatically. His numbers were encouraging, and definitely got us excited.

However, whenever a potential competitor is sharing information with you, you have to take everything with a grain of salt, as well as be careful how much you ask of them. It becomes inappropriate pretty fast to suggest they teach you how to compete with them. But his help did give us a good indication of what was possible and a good sense of the market.

One specific advantage we felt we had over Bacon Freak was that Rocco wasn't truly a web or branding guy. The three of us had been working in the industry for a long time, and we had the skills to build and deploy anything we could think of.

User-Experience Can Be a Product

WHEN IT COMES to user experience, everyone always mentions Apple, mainly because of the remarkable attention they pay to it. Apple makes every part of a purchase, down to the unboxing of the product, a joy. People write blog posts about what it's like to start a brand new Mac for the first time or pull a new iPod out of its box.

We decided early on that we had to do the same. Our brand had to embody the emotion we felt about bacon, and opening your package needed to live up to the excitement you felt as you prepared to feast on the country's best bacon. Each package we sent should be opened with excitement and joy, reminiscent of a seven-year-old on Christmas morning.

People could buy bacon in pretty much any grocery store, so if we expected them to pay up to three times more than they might have ever spent on bacon before, we had to deliver. And if we wanted them to come back, to tell their friends, we had to *kill* it. One of the ways in which we set out to accomplish this was through the manifestation of that user experience.

If you pay attention to those little details, your product becomes something people will talk about. If you really reward your customers, making the arrival of the mailman the best part of their day, they'll come back again and again. Your brand experience becomes part of the product they're buying. Whether you're selling downloadable software, a membership to an online club, or everyone's favorite cured meat, don't skimp out.

We also had experience with branding and story-telling, and had some fantastic graphic designers available to us. Rocco was clearly good at building a business, but we felt our site could sell the sex and sizzle of bacon a little better. Jason had worked at several agencies—and with clients worldwide—helping tell their brand stories online. Scott and Michael had built or could build whatever we needed. Between us, and hiring out what we couldn't do, we were confident that after Bac'n, the bacon world would never be the same.

SUPPLIERS AND EDIBILITY TESTING

Another brand decision was that we wanted our company to represent only the highest quality bacon and experience. Most people have plenty of options if they want bargain bacon, so that wouldn't be where our niche was. We needed to sell something that was unavailable in your local Wal-Mart—something that was worth paying a premium for. Our next step, therefore, had to be to find the best bacon we could.

We needed the kind of product that makes your eyes a little watery as they roll back in your head, and for just a minute, you don't breathe for fear of loosening some of that delicious flavor out of your mouth. We wanted the kind of bacon you ate dead last, so nothing would taint the soft aftertaste for as many minutes as you could keep it. We wanted life-changing bacon.

As we reached out to a few different bacon suppliers and farms, we were immediately received with a lot of excitement. Most of the farms had a very poor online presence, if any, and almost none of them took individual orders online. Most just didn't have the experience, interest, or capabilities to have a website and fulfill orders.

Just a little bit of bacon love from Broadbent

So when we came knocking, the door was answered with packages of free bacon. Most farms, including Beeler's and Broadbent and Scott's Hams, loved our idea and loved the thought of someone making their bacon available to their fans outside of their regular distribution. We started forming a pretty good relationship with all of them right off the bat.

And of course this meant weekends with PBR (or more formally, Pabst Blue Ribbon) and a camera as we cooked and tried the different bacons, photographed them, and in some instances, even filmed the cooking and eating and reviewing of the bacons. Let me just say it clearly: this is why you get in the business—a Sunday afternoon of eating three or four packages of bacon shared between three guys.

Somewhere, someone told Scott that orange juice was good to drink to offset the fat and grease and bacony goodness we were ingesting, so we drank glasses and glasses of the stuff to help diminish the damage we were doing to our bodies. Not sure it did much good, but we like to think it did.

■ Just another full plate of bacon and OJ

■ LAUNCH IN THREE WEEKS?

Leading up to Christmas 2008, the three of us had been talking quite a bit, but we really didn't have a strong game plan in place. We had talked with a few farms, found some great bacon that we knew we could carry, and were committed to building this site to see where it would take us, but we lacked that special something that kicks you into gear.

That thing became our bacon party.

■ Wouldn't you attend a party that was serving bacon sushi?

If we were going to throw an event centered around bacon, and if we were going to launch a company selling bacon, it seemed silly to not launch at the event. But we were going into heavy Christmas-holiday mode and that didn't leave us much time. However, as many people will tell you, some type of constraint—be it time or money or purpose—can do great things for motivation and creativity.

NOTE Setting a deadline you cannot move is an awesome way to motivate yourself.

We unanimously decided that immediately after Christmas we would get to work on Bac'n, and that we would launch on January 17th at our party. At this time, Scott and Michael were both working full-time at their day jobs, and Jason was doing freelance work, so evenings and weekends were cleared for the coming mayhem.

EVEN AGILE DEVELOPERS HAVE SOME KIND OF BUSINESS PLAN

Our goal was to launch quickly and adjust as necessary. We didn't want to spend too much time figuring out every detail, and speed was our asset.

But we also knew that not having a plan wasn't a responsible, well, plan.

What we did define for our plan was that we'd be selling bacon in individual packages as well as samplers. We wanted to help people decide which bacons to buy, and by offering a sampler at a small discount, we would encourage people to make larger orders without being overwhelmed by options. To start with, we had only a few: a sampler with a variety of our big bacon slabs, and a few that focused on the different farms where we were getting our bacon.

We also knew we'd try and build traffic through our blog, Twitter, Facebook, Adwords advertising, and with our bacn.me URL shortener. The blog would be a way for us to continue the blogging that Scott was doing for BaconGeek, and that Jason was helping out with on The Bacon Desk. We'd post interesting tidbits as well as talk about our products and share pictures, recipes, and coverage of events like our epic bacon-themed party.

■ Our Slab Sampler

Our goal was to get 2% conversion on our traffic, and to try and get as much free traffic as we could. We were also hoping to have a minimum order of $40, with an average margin of 40%. We knew from the start that the chance of earning enough revenue to put the three of us on payroll was pretty slim, but that was okay. Doing good work, even if it's not immediately financially lucrative, often offers much higher returns than doing nothing.

▓ SO, GET GOING

So with our small, assembled team, deadline in place, initial brand experience defined, and, oh yeah, some product we wanted to sell, the business was starting to come into focus. The only thing we needed at this point was to actually start building. Well—that and get a logo, and a design, and write all the content and… Holy shit. What did we sign up for? No time to talk, we better get going.

■ The three of us moments after we launched the site

chapter 2

FINDING THE BRAND

AS LONG AS my stapler staples, I really don't care that much about it. I don't care what brand it is, and I don't care about its logo, its color, or its packaging. I simply want my stapler to staple. And except for Milton from *Office Space*, I don't really know anyone who feels differently. For most of us, the stapler on our desk just isn't a part of our identity.

Bacon, on the other hand, is capable of being totally different. It's possible for bacon to just be food on a plate (think buffet bacon), we grant you that. However, it can be so much more.

Good bacon can be an experience. From the anticipatory moment you buy it at the store until the satisfied moment you've cleaned your frying pan, each interaction with bacon can be a moment of hope, and for some people, it is.

These people cherish bacon. They wear T-shirts, buy band-aids, eat mints, all proclaiming their love for bacon. They project their identity through the product.

When we set out to create a brand about bacon, we felt we owed it to our product to make that brand represent the goodness of what we were selling. We wanted to sell an experience that was cherished.

CHOOSING A NAME AND A DOMAIN

Our company name, Bac'n, came directly from our domain, bacn.com. Scott saw the opportunity to buy it and wasted no time. It was short, obvious (considering our main product), and fun.

From the beginning, though, we saw the purchase of the domain name as an investment rather than a straight cost. Our expectation was that if bacn.com needed to shut its doors someday, the domain would retain much of its value, if not more. Our brand, what it stood for, and the name, were all vital—and if there was one area to splurge on, it was getting the right domain.

Even though our domain was a huge asset, we also recognized that it presented some challenges. The first was that the term "bacn" already existed within Internet culture. According to Wikipedia, the phrase was initially coined in August of 2007 at PodCamp to refer to "electronic messages which have been subscribed to and are therefore not unsolicited but are often unread by the recipient for a long period of time, if at all. Bacn has been described as 'email you want but not right now.'"

This wasn't ideal. However, we all hated that definition and phrase, and felt it was something people had heard, but had never adopted. It was an orphaned phrase, ready for new application. We were happy to oblige.

Thoughts on Domain Names

IF YOU HAVEN'T named your company yet, look for available domain names first. There's nothing worse than thinking up a great name, but realizing all the interesting or brandable domains surrounding it are taken. We were pretty lucky to get a four-letter domain name, as those are pretty hard to come by. It's even more rare that it was a pronounceable domain that phonetically represented our product.

Clearly, this is why it was expensive, but also why we felt the domain itself was an investment. To someone buying a domain, if that domain has a history of content, inbound links, and a decent ranking, the value of the domain alone is increased, even if the site goes away. So we felt good about our decision to buy a quality domain from the beginning, because we planned on increasing that value over time.

Also, when buying a domain, we prefer short, simple domains whenever possible. Be careful about awkward spelling if it's a multi-word domain (repeating letters as the last and first letters of the words can be awkward to type and to look at). And make sure that two or more words, when crammed together, don't accidentally spell something else.

It's hard to find good, unregistered domains, so if you go with unusual words or spellings, really consider how hard or easy it will be to tell it to someone in a crowded room. If it takes more than three attempts to explain the spelling, it's a bad domain.

When searching for domains, we use ajaxwhois.com to quickly test availability on all the domains we can think of. Once we've narrowed them down, we buy them at GoDaddy.

The second problem we faced was that the term "bacon" didn't actually appear in our URL or name. This would make it much harder to organically rank in search engines for bacon-related searches. A keyword in the URL is a good sign of relevance. Also, people link to your site using your company name, which is part of Google's algorithm in determining ranking.

TIP If possible, you want your domain to contain the most relevant keyword within its name. While it's relatively easy to become the highest-ranked site for a unique word, what you want is to become the highest-ranked site for the product you're selling. If you want to buy shoes online and you already know where to look, you'll go to zappos.com, but if you search for the keyword "shoes," you'll see shoes.com and shoebuy.com first.

While not a catastrophic issue, we did recognize that our name would be a slight handicap.

A quick look at the sites ranking for the term "bacon" showed three things:

- Sir Francis Bacon had a lot of .edu websites talking about him, and they were going to rank very well as a result. This meant a search for just "bacon" would often suggest sites that had to do with Sir Francis Bacon. Little did he know so long ago that he'd be riding the bacon-meme coattails.

- Kevin Bacon wasn't as relevant as he used to be, but there are still a lot of sites talking about him and his degrees of separation.

- The rest of the bacon-related sites almost all had "bacon" in their URLs.

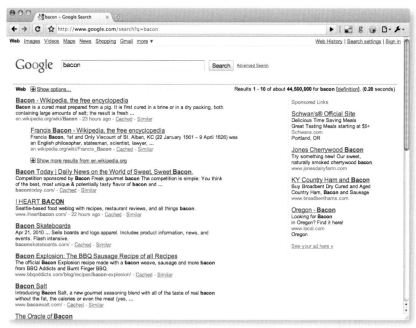

■ The Google search result for "bacon"

Sites like iheartbacon.com, bacontoday.com, baconskateboards.com, and baconunwrapped.com all ranked really well, and we were missing one of the keys to tap into that success.

Most search engines count links to your website as sort of a vote: the more links, the more votes, and thus the higher your rank in the search results. And the words that people use to link to your site influence the words for which your site will have a good rank. If every link has anchor text that uses the word "bacon," it's easier to rank for that term. At least that's the general idea.

NOTE Search engine optimization—aka the process of optimizing your site so that it ranks well in search engines for specific keywords—is actually the kind of thing that people write whole books and websites about. Aaron Wall is an industry leader in this area, and has a website and eBook available at SEObook.com.

However, because we didn't have that magical full word "bacon" in our name or URL, many of our links wouldn't add to our rank for "bacon." It was easy to get a high rank for "bacn"—we didn't have a lot of competition— but harder to move up the results list for "bacon." Still, we felt our brand opportunity and value in the short URL outweighed the negatives, and so we moved forward with the name Bac'n.

BUYING A DOMAIN NAME FROM A SQUATTER

When Scott began talking to Jason and Michael about coming on board, bacn.com was already registered by someone else. However, just because a site is registered doesn't mean it's not available, and a quick check of the actual site showed that it was a parked site. Some call this practice squatting; others call it holding an investment.

Scott had been looking around and talking with people about the brand name, and was researching what domains were out there. He'd spoken to Rocco at BaconFreak.com, who told him that bacon.com was currently owned by a domain holder who was asking $750,000 for it, after buying it for a third of that amount in the past. Clearly, that wasn't going to happen for us. The domain holder was also willing to lease the domain for a recurring payment, but even that was too expensive. So we kept looking for less expensive domains.

■ Bacon.com—just another ad-filled, parked domain

Eventually, Scott came to bacn.com. The address hosted a simple page announcing that the domain was for sale and listing a contact name and a price. It had apparently been bought as an investment, and it wasn't being used for a real site. Scott contacted the owner and threw out his own offer of about 50% of the asking price. When the owner countered with 60%, Scott accepted. Pretty painless. (It seems that while bacn.com was affordable, that single extra "o" in the name means quite a few zeros once it came to price.)

The next step in buying a domain owned by someone else is to bring in an escrow service—a company that holds the money until the domain transfer is final—and then the funds are released to the seller. The escrow service is a third-party company whose purpose is to make sure all goes as planned for both sides.

In this case, we used escrow.com. Initially, Scott was a bit wary of the service, as the site doesn't really look like a new, up-to-date website. It felt a bit dated, and didn't have the shiny logos or gradient buttons the web services we were used to using are known for. However, after asking around and looking at reviews online, we found it to be a reputable site, and it turned out to be great.

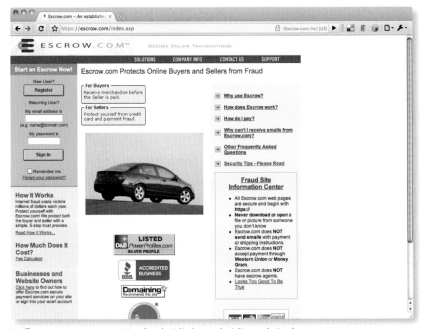

■ Escrow.com: not a pretty site, but it does what it needs to do.

After Scott submitted the funds and escrow.com confirmed the money was available, the owner of the domain transferred it to Scott's GoDaddy account. At that point, Scott confirmed the transfer and released the funds to the seller. From beginning to end, the process took about two weeks.

The lessons to be learned from this are to not be afraid of going after the perfect domain, even if it's already registered and being used by someone else. While new domains are tempting with their $8 price tag, the extra money spent on the right domain can have a worthwhile return on the investment. Also, many people who are holding a domain are motivated to sell. They would rather flip a domain for a small profit than watch the domain go un-purchased and continue to collect dust, so don't hesitate to contact them.

Finally, the price is always negotiable.

THE LOGO

We had a company name and a domain name, and now we needed an identity—specifically, a logo. A huge problem young companies face is that they want a really awesome logo and brand, but often lack the money to pay for the work upfront. Good design can be expensive, and shortcuts here can really hurt your company. But how do you come up with the money when you're bootstrapping the company and you haven't even launched yet? But launching with a half-assed logo is a sure-fire way to not get taken seriously. It's all so chicken and egg.

Jason's wife happened to be a graphic designer, but Jason was cautious and chose not to recommend her for the job. He hadn't known Scott or Michael for very long, and with Scott paying for the work out-of-pocket, Jason was concerned about appearance. He didn't want anyone thinking he was just trying to get his wife some work, even though she was a freelancer; and he didn't want it to be awkward if the design didn't match the team's standards or aesthetic—which happens. You're walking a fine line when you work with people you know and like while avoiding looking biased.

NOTE That said, if you're starting a company, and anyone in the startup has a spouse who happens to be a professional designer, don't be afraid to mention it. Really. Just throw it out there and see how people react. It would have saved Bac'n a bunch of time and money if we had gone with the easiest and most familiar option from the beginning.

Because Scott didn't know that Jason's wife was a designer, he asked around. More specifically, he posted his need to his followers on Twitter and quickly received a recommendation for a local Portlander from a friend whom he trusted. The designer was intrigued by the project, even though she was a vegan, and she thought the site idea was amusing, so she was willing to work within our budget.

Michael and Jason hadn't seen any of the designer's work beforehand, but Scott was moving fast and we both trusted him. We sent her some basic ideas about the brand: the logo should be fun but not goofy, cool but still professional. We wanted it to be interesting and aspirational. And most importantly, it had to look better than the majority of the other bacon-related sites out there—a problem we didn't anticipate being an issue.

NOTE An aspirational brand is one that elevates a product, makes it something special or unique. "In consumer marketing," says Wikipedia, an aspirational brand (or product) means "... a large segment of its exposure audience wishes to own it, but for economical reasons cannot. An aspirational product implies certain positive characteristics to the user, but the supply appears limited due to limited production quantities." We would also add that an aspirational brand is one that leads the market. It also portrays characteristics that the consumer personally aspires toward.

I'm not exactly sure why, but we had found during our research that bacon-related websites tended to be terribly designed. Many had hokey, default blog themes, and others just looked thrown together by people taking a crash course in beginner's HTML. We wanted Bac'n to stand out, to be aspirational, to replicate that emotional experience that people encounter with bacon.

Working with Designers on a Budget

THERE'S NOTHING WRONG with having a small design budget, and it is absolutely possible to get fantastic results without spending all of your pre-launch marketing dollars. However, here are a few things to keep in mind as you work with designers.

- Most importantly, never ever ever promise future cash rewards for work done for free right now. This is insulting to the designer, their profession, and your company. If you want design work done, you should be willing to pay for it now. Even though you're sure your company is going to be huge, and you know you could more than make up for it later, designers need to get paid on time for their work.

- You may offer equity in your company in exchange for work, including design work. This is very different from the promise of payment later. It's *equity*. However, your designer is now a partner, not just a designer, so don't forget to treat him or her as such.

- Never offer to pay a designer less because you're providing a really great opportunity for him or her to build a portfolio. I've never met a designer who was looking for portfolio pieces more than money. If you do find one, awesome, but never assume it. In fact, never mention it. If they are looking, they'll let you know.

- It's important to remember that designers don't "owe" you anything. A lot of people treat designers as if they—the designers, that is—should be thanking them on their knees because this company is willing to give them paying work. That is just wrong. Designers are professionals and deserve to be treated as such. They probably don't need you nearly as much as you need them.

(continues on next page)

Working with Designers on a Budget (continued)

- If you really need to lower the cost of design, you may have to give up some element of control. I've seen a lot of projects become more and more expensive because the client tries to over-manage the designer. Give your designer very clear, specific instruction early on. Tell them exactly what you are looking for, provide examples you like, and tell them why. Then let them go and create something. There will be times when you may not like what they come back with, but ask yourself if this is a personal preference, or truly a poor design. If you can't afford an expensive logo, consider removing your emotions and desires, and just let a good designer come back with a good logo, accept it, and move on. If you want 3–5 rounds of revisions and lots of options with your final and absolute control, expect to pay for all of that.

- If you have a limited budget, commission only the designs you need right away. If your business is a website, you probably don't need letterhead and business cards the first day. Start with as few items as possible, saving the designer's hours for when you really need them.

- Finally, for the truly tiny budget, consider working with graphic design students from your local college or university. Many students are dying to make design their job, and it's far more rewarding to get paid to design a logo while in school than deliver pizza. However, you should still strictly adhere to the rules above. Just because your designer is a student does not diminish his or her right to be treated as a professional and enter into appropriate business agreements.

After a few days, the designer sent Scott some really rough concepts, basically a broad overall direction with her thoughts. After reviewing the concepts with his wife, Kami, Scott sent back some suggestions. Some of their feedback was even done by sketching up their response on a dry-erase board and sending photos from their phone. Within another day or so, we got a more formal first round of comps showcasing about 13 different ideas and iterations.

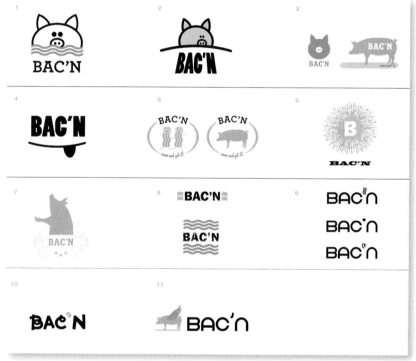

■ The first batch of logos, back from the designer

Some of the logos resonated, and felt like they were close, and some were not what we were looking for at all. Between a few emails and phone calls, we started getting a feel for our collective response. All of us liked one or two different ideas, and there were a few that we all thought were cool; but there wasn't one logo that really just captured us—nothing that told us "THIS is the icon of your brand" and nothing that just said "DAMN, we HAVE to use this."

Scott kept going back to one specific comp. It was a small, simple half-circle of a pig face, peeking over an arching horizon, eyes looking off in the distance. Scott was digging on it, and continued to bring it up during our conversations. "There's just something about this little guy," he would say, and we'd all look at it and agree. We liked the slightly mischievous nature of the character, and the simplicity of the drawing. However, it didn't feel strong enough to be Bac'n's identity. It was cute, but not awesome. It couldn't be the face of the Bacon Capitol of the World.

■ So... mischievous

Jason, on the other hand, liked the last design of the batch. It was a simple outline of a pig, bearing a slight shadow and a large protruding wing. It reminded him of the Simpsons episode where Lisa tells Homer that pork, bacon, and ham all come from the same animal. Homer's response, "Right, Lisa, some wonderful, magical animal!?"

 NOTE Homer Simpson is a noted bacon fan—so much so that the Royal Bacon Society, another bacon-themed blog, created a top-ten list from his bacon quotes. Of course, this one was number one.

The idea of a magical animal just sounded awesome. Jason imagined creating a mythical animal from this winged pig, a magical creature that was made only of bacon. It seemed like it would be a lot of fun to create a mythology around Bac'n and its mascot. The other guys laughed, and kind of saw what he was going after, but in the end, it didn't make the cut either.

■ Winged and magical

The more we talked, the more we realized that there was something specific missing from the designs. The designer was good, but the aesthetic we really wanted wasn't being captured in her designs. And because we didn't have much time, and even less money, we voted to pull the plug and try a different designer.

Now, Jason's wife is a good graphic designer who'd worked at a prestigious agency in Portland doing branding work. So at this point of desperation, Jason finally discarded his fears of being inappropriate and suggested her.

Looking back … hindsight and all that … Jason was way off in his notion of how his partnering co-founders would respond to this suggestion. Both Michael and Scott were stoked about the idea of having someone "in-house" to do the work, and now that Jason knew Scott better, he knew Scott wouldn't have cared even if Jason had tried to shill his wife for the job. As long as Bac'n got a good product in the end, it didn't really matter how we got there or who did the work.

So, with that information filtering in, Jason approached his wife.

NOTE OK, there was one other reason Jason didn't approach Holly first. They have kind of a standing rule not to work together. It's just better for their marriage. However, in this case we were desperate, and Jason knew she had it in her. But working with spouses can be tricky, especially when one is giving the direction and the other is doing the work. Throw in the passion and emotional pressure of this being a personal project, and it was understandable he was hesitant.

Within a couple of days we got an initial set of directions from Holly.

▨ LEARNED LESSONS IN BRANDING

We should back up a bit and acknowledge that moving from one designer to another mid-project is a very difficult decision, not to mention a delicate dance to avoid hurt feelings and burnt bridges. Of the three of us, Jason had the most experience with branding and design, and felt he needed to take the lead. He also knew that for this project, we weren't getting what we wanted. However, to change course mid-way you have to be pretty sure, and you'd better be right the second time.

The first part of the decision was telling the original designer. We were honest in that we really liked some of her ideas, but explained that we had a different feel in mind and that her adjustments didn't seem like they were going to come far enough. Obviously, we paid her for her time and made sure that we now owned the rights to whatever she had drawn up. If you don't finish a project with someone, there's no guarantee that you own the partial work, so we were very clear with that and we all agreed that her work was now our property. In the end, we believe she was paid well for her time, and we all learned something. It was unfortunate, but not the worst experience we've come across, or come up against ourselves.

But the next thing we did had a huge benefit. We went back and really defined—explicitly—what our brand goals were, and specified some of the use cases we were most excited about. For instance, we knew we wanted T-shirts for our brand, and so the logo had to look great on a T-shirt. We loved the idea of wrapping all of our bacon in butcher paper (even the pre-packaged bacon would get additionally wrapped in butcher paper), and the outside of that paper should host a big stamp of our brand. We wanted the experience of opening a box from Bac'n to be a beautiful mix of Christmas morning and fresh-from-the-butcher-shop excitement.

And in clarifying these decisions, we also realized that the design needed to be heavy and substantial—it couldn't be light or airy. And it needed to be cool even if people didn't know what it was.

It was about this time that we also started talking about adding a tagline to the brand, and again pulling from his pop-culture past, Jason mentioned the most popular bacon quote of all time, "Bacon tastes good," as spoken by Vincent Vega in *Pulp Fiction*. We decided that our brand and tagline would be "Bac'n—tastes good."

We then handed off this newly distinct direction to Jason's wife, Holly, feeling like we had learned a lot from our previous mistake, and now holding a much better idea of not only our brand, but our entire identity. What before was merely "fun, but not goofy," now was "strong and stable." It should look great as a T-shirt, and it should look great as a stamp. If it didn't look like it could come out of a butcher shop, it was wrong. Oh, and make it f'ing cool.

PHASE TWO: A NEW DIRECTION

Exactly a week after we got the first designs back from the first designer, we were getting the first designs back from the second designer. They couldn't have been more different, and immediately we felt like we were on the right track.

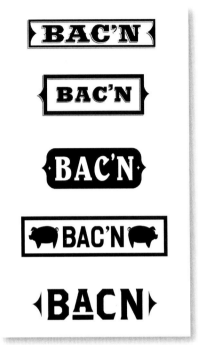

■ Definitely different, and going in the right direction

We each had our favorites, but all of us recognized that any of these would do. We picked the most popular, and asked for a few different approaches to it. We wanted to see it without a drop shadow and a stronger stroke so it would work on both a T-shirt or on the website at a small size.

At this point we also showed Holly the designs that the first designer had done, and mentioned our overall appreciation of the simple pig profile. Because she was Jason's wife, she was able to ask lots of questions as she had much more access to Jason and his free time than someone working remotely. All of this really helped us give succinct feedback, which in turn gave us a better product.

Then Holly came back with the second round of designs and Jason sent them off to the other guys for their thoughts. But as soon as we saw them, we all knew we were done. There wasn't any more work to do, or tweaks necessary. We were openly in agreement, set upon the design we now have.

■ See that one on the right? Yeah, it's our logo.

Looking back, none of us can imagine a different design for Bac'n. It's so clearly the right mark for us, and defines who we are so well. It has also become an incredibly popular T-shirt, selling hundreds of shirts with only our logo. It's a pretty great feeling when the logo for your company becomes a design people want to wear as a T-shirt. It's even more impressive when the visual isn't an iconic fashion brand, but just a small company selling bacon. And every time any of us wears one of these shirts in public, it's a good bet it'll get a comment.

KEY TAKEAWAYS

As you read through our process, it's pretty obvious we made some mistakes. We were woefully unprepared when we started talking to our first designer, and we did her a great disservice by not properly identifying our brand goals and vision to begin with. Jason continues to take full responsibility for that mistake (and Scott tells him to get over it), and as a result he's probably over-communicated his desires and expectations with more recent projects.

Also, we didn't do enough research to make sure we were getting the right designer. Designers have very different aesthetics, and we started with one whose style didn't match our brand from the beginning. We chose her originally because we were on a tight budget, and she was willing to work with us. However, we would have saved money in the long run by working with the right designer, and using less of her time, to begin with.

Finally, we learned that you don't have to love everything a designer does, and in the most extreme circumstances you can even change designers. However, it's critical to treat your designers with respect, be upfront, honest, and fair with them at all times. Who knows, they might be the perfect designer for your next project.

 Resources

- Ajaxwhois: http://ajaxwhois.com/
- GoDaddy: http://godaddy.com
- Wikipedia.org: http://en.wikipedia.org/wiki/Bacn_%28electronic%29
- SEO Book: http://seobook.com
- Escrow.com: http://escrow.com
- Simpson's Quote: http://www.royalbaconsociety.com/blog/funny-bacon/top-10-bacon-quotes-from-homer-simpson

chapter 3

BUILDING BAC'N

WITH ONLY THREE weeks to build the site, we knew we had to make a few compromises. There was just no way we were going to be able to do enough planning, to have the luxury of multiple design rounds for the site, nor even to build all the functionality we'd want. We also knew that we were going to have to take every possible shortcut, and this meant using every possible web service and startup out there with services aimed at making our jobs easier.

In the past couple of years, endless startups have been created trying to solve small production problems. The big ones are sites like WordPress or Blogger, which allow you to create, launch, and publish a blog in minutes.

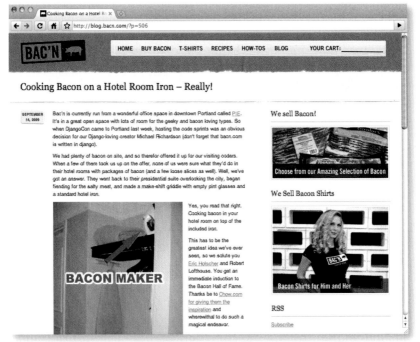

■ The Bac'n Blog, in all its WordPress glory

There are also companies that offer hyper-specific tools like JS-Kit (now called Echo), which we used for the sole function of providing the ability for users to comment on our site. Whether those comments are in the blog itself, or in normal product pages, Echo allows any site to contain feedback forms just by adding a small piece of HTML to your code.

The products and services of these startups range in price from completely free to varying degrees of pay models. Most are affordable, powerful, and simple to integrate into your site. In this chapter we'll look at a few that we used, their competitors, and our experience using them.

OFF THE SHELF

Even though we weren't making the world's most complex site, we still needed some specific functionality in terms of content management. We knew we wanted to have different product types (bacon, shirts, etc.), and we wanted to have different content types (recipes, how-to videos, product overviews, etc.). We also wanted to customize the specific fields available to us for each content type, and determine how the content would be displayed.

We could have chosen from among plenty of options for this task, but when you're looking for solutions, you have to balance features with the real cost of the software or the time it takes to become proficient at using it. There wasn't a pre-existing, off-the-shelf solution that would allow us the flexibility we needed while also being something Michael could immediately dive into, and we didn't have the time for him to learn a new platform just for this site. He really wanted to continue building using the Django platform, so we took advantage of that desire, and set him loose to create our own CMS.

▩ CONTENT MANAGEMENT SYSTEM— DJANGO WEB FRAMEWORK

Django is a web development platform built on the programming language Python. The most important thing to know about Django is that the "D" is silent. You'll look like a big n00b if you pronounce it, so don't.

Web development frameworks have become very popular by creating and providing prebuilt tools and functionality that a programmer can call upon while coding a site. For instance, rather than have to build a user account system every time you make a site with user accounts, you can merely write code that calls the framework's user library, and the framework will build the user account system for you. You can still customize the account system if needed, but much of the time you can use the library's previously written code to immediately get 90% of the functionality you need. Clearly, this saves a lot of time, and as frameworks continue to gain adoption, they are growing in complexity and capability.

Literally, Making Our Own Bacon

ONE OF THE things that got Scott going on the whole bacon craze was the idea of making his own bacon. He found a blog post from the folks over at BSBrewing.com titled "Makin Bacon" that showed all of the details on how to make, smoke, and prepare your own bacon. They gave step-by-step instructions, complete with compelling photos of the process. The end product, so delicious, was just too much to resist.

Scott set about smoking his own bacon with a slab of pork belly from his local butcher shop. It took him a good week to make, but it was an awesome experience, and something that really connected him to the pork product. Once you've made your own bacon, you've moved into an elite group of people who are personally qualified to discuss (and sell) bacon. Building a site selling bacon was the logical next step.

■ Prepping the pork belly

■ The belly, waiting on the rack to be smoked

■ Getting warmer...The finished, super-thick product

One of the more popular frameworks is Ruby on Rails, created by 37signals partner David Heinemeier Hansson. 37signals used it during the development of their online tools, including Basecamp and Campfire. These tools gave a lot of credibility to the idea of frameworks to allow for fast, iterative programming.

Michael knew Django, so that's what we used, but we could have used any of the frameworks. There are frameworks for PHP, Ruby, Python—pretty much any modern language. They are open-source, and free, so they're an easy choice for modern developers. Some have different reputations for being better or worse than others depending on the task, so you should research the strengths and weaknesses of any specific language and framework before you get started. There are lots of user groups based on these frameworks, so look around in your community and see if there's a group near you to get involved with.

BLOG—WORDPRESS

We wanted a fairly traditional blog for the site as well, and while Django could have given us a basic, functional blog within its framework, hosted blogs and off-the-shelf solutions were so powerful and easy to use it didn't make sense not to use a dedicated tool for the job.

When the site launched, we didn't have a ton of time to customize the blog, so we went with Tumblr for launch day. It's a great tool for sharing a stream of photos, videos, short posts, and quotes. It's easy to use, and free.

However, the functionality is somewhat limited—at least compared with WordPress, which is the reigning champ in terms of open-source blog platforms. WordPress is a rich, powerful, extensible tool that has been used in such a variety of ways, it's hard to imagine what it can't do. Jason was very familiar with it, as well as with extending its core functionality through plugins (such as the All-In-One SEO Pack), and wanted to be able to set up galleries and style the blog exactly like the rest of the Bac'n site.

■ Filling out these three fields is all you need to have a Tumblr blog.

Tumblr allowed us to launch on Day 1 with something, but as soon as there was time, Jason went in and customized a WordPress installation to manage our blog.

 Familiarity

WITH SO MANY options out there, and new ones coming into existence every day, it's very easy to get distracted comparing advanced features and options and finding yourself paralyzed over features that really won't affect your bottom line.

Wasting 20 hours finding a slightly better tool and learning to use it only to gain a feature that saves you 10 minutes is a poor tradeoff. Rather than agonizing over which tools to choose, we used ones we already knew. This enabled us to extract much greater efficiencies by doing tasks that had a large return on investment, such as writing content and reviewing more products.

Remember, a key feature in finding and choosing tools is familiarity. If one tool does what you need it to, and you know how to use it, then often it's best to just use that tool. You can always change later if needed.

SHOPPING CART—GOOGLE CHECKOUT

When we built Bac'n, there were very few options for a shopping cart that would be easy to use and allow for simple setup, customization, and integration into our site. We consulted our network of peers, and no one had a decent tool to recommend. Because it had to integrate seamlessly into the site, we decided to go with the best option we could find, Google Checkout.

Google Checkout has some amazing functionality built in and it allows you to integrate a plethora of options and other tools to make a powerful system in a short amount of time. It has a really nice, simple, web-based admin for tracking orders, entering shipping information, calculating shipping on the fly, and so on. It's also affordable; the product is free, and Google charges only a small percentage when people actually place an order. (That's a typical model for hosted solutions.)

With Google Checkout, we were able to set prices and any other product information in our Django-built CMS and have it auto-feed quickly and easily into Google's checkout process. And we were able to incorporate a site-wide shopping cart, meaning people could add a product to their cart and continue on to any other page in the site while always being just one click away from checking out. Some other shopping carts offer subdomain solutions, where you have to be at store.domain.com in order to see or interact with your shopping list, which sometimes is fine, but wasn't ideal for our content-heavy site.

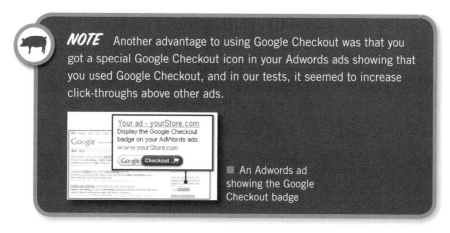

NOTE Another advantage to using Google Checkout was that you got a special Google Checkout icon in your Adwords ads showing that you used Google Checkout, and in our tests, it seemed to increase click-throughs above other ads.

An Adwords ad showing the Google Checkout badge

For the most part, it seemed that Google Checkout was an awesome solution. However, once we launched, we learned from our users that not everybody loves Google and their solve-the-world's-problems approach. We got several requests from users to offer an additional method of payment, and we found that many of our customers were people who had to create a new Google account just to order from us. We hadn't realized that users must have a Google account to use Google Checkout, and even if we had known, we wouldn't have thought it would be a problem, as everyone we know has a Google account. Unfortunately, that kind of misperception can happen when you work in a tech bubble, and the rest of the world quickly informed us that not everyone has, or wants, a Google account.

Looking back, we regret that we didn't try another checkout solution, or provide other options to users who didn't like or want to use Google Checkout. But we'll be honest about why we didn't: the reality is, we had a hard time getting excited about doing the work.

Incorporating shopping-cart software is a pain in the ass and once the site was live, we had already solved the interesting problems. It wasn't like the site was broken or not working; this was an incremental improvement in user experience. When we considered changing things, we had to battle against the reality that the momentum and the excitement of the project was gone.

Google Checkout worked. It may not have been perfect, but it did the job. And the effort to change cart software would have been significant, based only on the premise that it would increase orders, but with no clear idea by how much. So, we stuck with Google Checkout.

Guilty as Charged

LOSING MOMENTUM WHEN the fun of starting up has passed is a problem we've encountered several times with other people and on other projects, and we readily admit that we've been guilty of it ourselves. The initial excitement of a project can carry you through a lot of the miserable parts of a job, but once that excitement is gone, it's much tougher to go back and invest a lot of time in an incremental improvement. Had the three of us been working together in an office, we don't think it would have been as big of an issue. But when the work has to be done over a weekend, by yourself, with little excitement or appreciation, motivation can be a factor. It's worth being aware of, and oftentimes addressing it and recognizing it for what it is can help you move through it.

USER COMMENTS AND FEEDBACK—ECHO

For the primary site content we used a custom Django-built content management solution (CMS), and for the blog, we used WordPress. The blog was put on a subdomain, blog.bacn.com, to make it easier to manage and edit, and it allowed us to have two different servers with different settings for each. Most people probably don't need this level of sophistication, but it wasn't extra work for us, so we went with it.

Having the content in two different areas and with two different platforms did create a technical problem when it came to allowing users to leave feedback on the site. We wanted people to be able to comment and rate our products, but how could we create a uniform system across what were essentially two different sites?

We initially looked at GetSatisfaction, a fantastic hosted app that provides feedback and commenting tools. However, we realized it was better suited for software development; its ratings and bug tools weren't necessary for our specific needs.

Then we looked at Echo, and recognized that it solved our problem in an elegant and easy-to-implement solution. We were able to put a small snippet of code in all areas of the site where we wanted feedback, and users throughout the site would have a consistent experience. A WordPress plugin allowed the commenting through Echo to be seamlessly integrated with WordPress's comment tools. And we could allow users the ability to rate our bacon products using a five-star system and/or leave a comment for each product individually.

■ We also used UserVoice to create a popup feedback widget throughout the site

IntenseDebate boasts many of the same features as Echo, and has been acquired by Automattic, the makers of WordPress. The feature sets of the two products are similar enough that in the end, our decision to go with Echo was almost arbitrary. It did what we needed and it was the first tool we looked at that met all our needs. When deadlines are short, just making a decision is often more valuable than making the slightly better decision, but we're not sure we could have made a wrong choice here. Either product would have worked.

THE BUYING EXPERIENCE

Once we had decided which tools would allow us to assemble the site as quickly as possible, it was time to actually start assembling. A key question we had to answer to our own satisfaction was what content would we have on the site, and how the content would impact sales. Selling bacon online could be an average experience—one of factual information and a few images—or it could be fun and interesting, hopefully creating content that users loved regardless of their intention to buy bacon. To that end, we knew we wanted to do all we could to make the experience unique.

KEEP 'EM WATCHING

One of the ways we decided to help make the experience unique was that every product we had on the site should have a video accompanying it.

The videos were often simple reviews of the product, taken at one of our houses as we cooked and ate the product. We'd take exhaustive photos during the cooking process (many of which are in this book), and filmed using a combination handheld camcorder and a Nikon D90 DSLR camera that also shoots HD video. We were purposefully lo-fi in our approach, and most of the time only had one take per video. While we may not be the three most handsome or charming guys in town, we felt we were perfect for the straightforward geekiness of a site that sold bacon. That freed us to have fun, be ourselves, and just talk about great bacon as we filmed and ate. If one of us cussed, so what, and there wasn't a single shoot that didn't involve at least a couple of PBRs, even when we started pretty early in the morning. You can often see stray cans in our videos, which we never staged, but never edited out either.

■ Jason and Michael discuss the delicate intricacies of filming bacon.

Our videos added a lot to the site by keeping people interested for longer, and as we captured their attention, we had a better chance of capturing their business as well. Later in the year, Scott was actually flown to San Francisco to reshoot many of the videos with Chow.com, which was acquired in 2009 by CBS Interactive. They took our "How to make the perfect BLT" video along with a few others and shot them in their amazing studio. Those videos were then featured on Chow.com, as well as sent to the Checkout Network, appearing at checkout stands around the country. It's fun to think that the videos made over spare bacon and PBR became content for shoppers around the country as they waited to buy their groceries, perhaps even some bacon.

In the videos, we also tried to share bacon knowledge. We had several videos discussing the various ways to cook bacon (the "slow and low," "stir," and "broil" techniques all offer varying results and advantages), and we covered Basic Bacon 101 with videos outlining the differences between smoked, country, or uncured bacon. We like to think our videos were a lot of fun and added a ton of character to the site.

■ Scott's video playing on Chow.com

To host the videos, we originally used Vimeo. Vimeo allows for beautiful, high-def streaming and really focuses on the user experience and on maintaining quality. At the time, neither Google nor YouTube allowed for HD-quality videos, and the other options were far inferior to Vimeo.

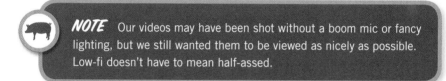

NOTE Our videos may have been shot without a boom mic or fancy lighting, but we still wanted them to be viewed as nicely as possible. Low-fi doesn't have to mean half-assed.

But Vimeo doesn't allow commercial videos on its site. We knew this at the time, but decided to believe that our content wasn't actually selling our bacon, but was selling the values of bacon in general. We also saw several other companies using the site, so we went ahead and used the service.

And it worked.

For a while.

In August, 2009, we were contacted and asked to remove our content from Vimeo and informed that our account would be closed. We tried to appeal, stating that our content, while produced with commercial intent, was really universal information and valuable outside of commercial purposes. It didn't work, and within a week our videos were moved to another service called Viddler.

We didn't feel bad about our decision, and would do it again if necessary. For eight months we got to use the service we preferred and that offered the best experience. Even though we use a different service now, we had a good run using the best service possible. And by the time we had to move our content, other services, such as Viddler, were offering HD streaming video.

■ AUXILLARY SITE CONTENT

Other content we added to the site came directly from our epic bacon-themed party (see Chapter 5). With more than 40 people each bringing a delicious dish featuring bacon, we had a great supply of starting recipes for bacn.com. We even had some really great photography thanks to Scott and his always-on camera during the event.

> *NOTE* Even with the thousands and thousands of websites out there featuring recipes, recipes continue to be a really great source of organic traffic.

■ One of the entries—yes, that's really bacon maple custard pie.

We listed the recipes and created a well-designed page to showcase the instructions. We could have done more than we did, especially in terms of listing the recipes and filtering and searching within them or adding photographs, but the point of the site wasn't to get people great recipes, it was to sell great bacon, so we kept that part of the site simple and hoped people would make their way to buying rather than just browsing the recipes section.

■ The Bacon Maple Custard Pie recipe page

THE SITE DESIGN

As we finalized much of the content and its form, and as Michael built the site and assembled its third-party tools, we needed to turn our in-progress branding into the actual HTML and images for the website itself. Our logo was finished, but we were only a week away from launch and didn't have a site design yet.

Scott suggested we approach Darin Richardson of Refresh Media, and Darin agreed to design the site on a budget, on a timeline, and to be paid after the site launched (and some of the agreed payment would be in bacon). We know—this breaks almost every rule we spelled out so loudly in the previous chapter. But Scott and Darin had a long, positive history, and over the years, Scott had sent Darin a lot of business through personal referrals and evangelizing Refresh Media, and Darin liked what we were doing and agreed to help us as a favor.

We were asking Darin to deliver a design on a very tight deadline, but one great thing about Darin was that he was more than a designer. He was also a web developer. This meant that we could trust him to be aware of development details, and that he would be able to hand off design in finished and tested HTML.

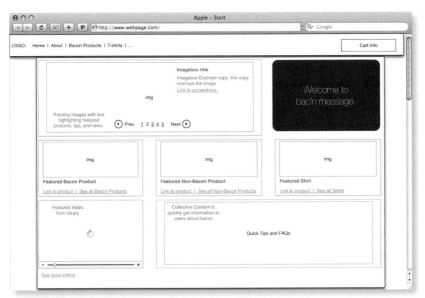

■ Our wireframe for the homepage. Notice that there are content boxes and notes about function, but no real design decisions or production decisions made? This allows the designer to know what they're designing, and to have a strong sense of content and function as they work through their own decisions.

Jason met with Darin and showed him some simple wireframes that dictated the content we'd have, its basic hierarchy of importance, and how we wanted people to move within the site. We knew we were asking him to deliver a design in a very tight deadline, and we needed the designs to come in ready to go. Having wireframes—even though these weren't complex pages—allowed Darin to move even quicker. And with Darin delivering designs in HTML, we could move right into implementation.

The Importance of a Designer-Developer

IT'S ALMOST IMPOSSIBLE to exaggerate the value of working with someone who understands web development as well as design. With a fantastic designer who doesn't regularly do interactive design work, tons of small and seemingly insignificant details might get overlooked. For instance, if you sign up for a newsletter and enter your email address, what happens after you hit submit? What happens if there is an error? What happens if that email address is already in the database?

These decisions may seem small or insignificant, but if you hand over a design without having made them, there's a good chance they'll be decided in whatever way is easiest for the programmer. A good designer will think of these things and provide design direction for them ahead of time.

And when a good designer who's also a developer does the HTML markup, there's a good chance the HTML will be a pixel-perfect match to the design. I've worked with programmers who don't necessarily have an eye for things like kerning, letter spacing, or other typographic details, and after the developer builds the site, it loses a little of that special something that the designer was able to fashion. Much of a designer's craft comes from small and subtle touches, and it's easy for an untrained eye to miss them (or their importance). A good designer/developer who provides HTML will often be more compulsive about those details than you may think is necessary, but be happy if that happens—the HTML will come in perfect, ready to go. It's a huge asset—especially when time is an issue—to not have to go back and forth between these sometimes-separate vendors.

The first time we saw the initial comp for the site design was five days before the site was to launch. Fortunately for us, it was awesome. Our changes were more about integrating than actually making any alterations. We loved it completely and from the beginning.

Darin was an absolute champ through and through, and he met with Michael on the evenings leading up to the launch and helped us not only modify a few things for the design, but also worked with us to incorporate his HTML into our content management system templates.

Of all the things that could have derailed our launch, the design and implementation led the list. While we got away with getting great service affordably, it should be said that we'll never settle for sub-par design work or vendors after that experience. Working with a professional like Darin saved the launch, and we're convinced it's worth whatever it takes to only work with people like him in the future.

 ## Resources

- Django: http://www.djangoproject.com
- Ruby on Rails: http://rubyonrails.org
- Makin Bacon at BS Brewing: http://www.bsbrewing.com/blog/2007/08/makin-bacon/
- WordPress: http://wordpress.org
- All-in-One SEO Pack: http://semperfiwebdesign.com
- Tumblr: http://tumblr.com
- Google Checkout: http:// checkout.google.com
- Uservoice: https://uservoice.com
- Get Satisfaction: http://getsatisfaction.com
- Intense Debate: http://intensedebate.com
- Refresh Media: http://refreshmedia.com
- Chow.com: http://www.chow.com/stories/11779
- Vimeo: http://vimeo.com
- Viddler: http://viddler.com

chapter 4

LOGISTICS (OR THE SITE ISN'T EVERYTHING)

WE CARRIED INVENTORY, and we shipped bacon. People didn't believe us at first, but we did. We stored it in refrigerators inside garages and in our office. We got it from supply centers and direct from the farms. We packed it in ice packs inside insulated cold shields and shipped it via USPS.

We could have used a shipping facility, or found a place that would drop-ship for us, but we didn't. We figured just selling bacon wasn't interesting. We wanted to create a brand and a product. And since we weren't making the bacon, we had to create something else.

So we shipped an experience. A wrapped-in-butcher-paper-goodness experience that people wanted to tell their friends about. An experience that, as with any excellent gift-giving experience, we wanted to receive in the mail ourselves. And in the beginning, the only way to affordably create this experience was not only to be in charge but to do every step ourselves.

When we started, we really didn't know what we were getting into by actually deciding to do inventory and fulfillment. And we really didn't know how it would work, we just figured, "Scott has a big garage, we can deal with it later." This *may* have been a bit naïve.

SHIPPING SUPPLIES

When we saw what other people were doing in the bacon niche, it was obvious we could do better. Most of the products and brands were hastily thrown together, and few seemed to be shooting for true customer loyalty. And while we believed in our ability to create loyalty, we still had to get the logistics worked out.

For us to be successful, we had to figure out a) boxes, b) shipping material, c) actual postage, and of course d) delivery to point-of-shipping.

At first we went highbrow. We looked at companies that would make custom boxes for us, with our logos and message right on the side of the box. But that's pretty expensive when you're not buying in massive volume, so we had to put that on the "someday-maybe" list.

Then we looked at offerings from FedEx and UPS, but they all seemed to fall short of our needs; they were expensive and kind of painful to deal with. Eventually we looked into the USPS and realized it was a no-brainer.

Did you know that USPS flat-rate shipping is amazing? It's cheap and you get free boxes. Let me repeat that. *YOU GET FREE BOXES.* It sounds trivial, but when you're buying all of your shipping products, and spending hundreds of dollars on things like ice packs and heat shields just to send someone something, free boxes are awesome.

USPS has a flat-rate priority mail shipping method that gives you three options for boxes. You can fit up to 70 pounds in them, although in practice we rarely put in more than 20. Once we saw this, we knew USPS was the way to go.

WRAPPIN' IT ALL UP

We placed orders for many of the different bacon-themed products on the Internet, and found that most of the companies didn't put much time in their actual shipping experience. You got a box with a Mylar envelope, and inside was a bunch of bacon and cold packs. It was a little anti-climactic. We wanted to deliver something a little more fun, and more on brand.

In early conversations, Jason had mentioned the idea of offering a butcher-via-the-Internet experience to our customers. The idea was to take one of those Mylar envelopes (that we unfortunately really needed to keep our bacon cold as it shipped) and wrap it with butcher paper and then stamp it with a big Bac'n logo.

We felt it was something our customers would appreciate, mainly because it's how we would have wanted our bacon to come in the mail.

If you've never seen a Mylar envelope, it looks like a missing piece from some robot-from-the-future costume. It's terrible.

■ The unboxing of one of our competitor's uninspiring bacon packages

However, when you take the bacon, wrap it up in a giant sheet of butcher paper, and seal it with a nice big Bac'n sticker, you start to get closer to a true butcher-shop experience. Stamping our logo on top gave it a physical, old-school feel that we felt made the experience a bit more enjoyable.

■ Just think of us as your friendly Internet butcher shop.

■ DESIGN EVERYTHING—EVEN PACKING SLIPS

We loved our logo and wanted it on everything we sent, so we formatted it for different stickers and sent them off to get printed at StickerGiant.com. We had two different stickers made, one of just our logo and another of simple instructions that helped our customers understand how to keep their bacon fresh and whether or not to be worried if their cured and smoked bacon showed up at room temperature. (Hint: You're fine. It's more aesthetically pleasing cold, but cured bacon can be stored at room temperature.)

We used these stickers as giveaways at events as well, and as a way to seal the butcher paper itself. Again, all part of the experience.

■ The stickers let buyers know their room-temperature, cured bacon was a-okay.

With most packages you get in the mail, it's common to see some plain white packing slip made with a generic template. It usually looks like it was printed on some default template from Word. However, we saw this as another opportunity to push the branding, so again, Jason's wife whipped up a great-looking packing slip that Michael was easily able to integrate into the fulfillment process.

"YES! BAC'N IS HERE!" What a welcome sight. After all, who isn't excited about getting bacon in the mail? We also made sure to not include any of the pricing information (just what they got and the quantities) on the packing slip so folks could send it as a gift.

> **NOTE** Looking back, we wish we had offered more tools for folks to send bacon as a gift, based on the feedback we got from customers during our first Christmas. Having tools to customize messages on the packing slip would have been a nice touch.

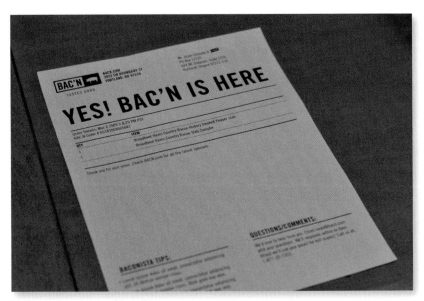

■ Our exclamatory packing slip

For all of our shipping supplies, we went to uline.com. ULINE was great for things like cold packs, butcher paper, Mylar envelopes, and so on. Not only that, since we had to order a bunch of stuff from the start, we gang-shipped a lot of it and lowered our initial shipping costs for our shipping supplies (ironic, we know). Ideally we would have sourced all of that stuff locally, because 1000 cold packs aren't cheap to ship, but it was hard for us to find those materials in large quantities where we lived, so we went with ULINE.

STORING THE BACON

In the first few months after launch, we were keeping inventory of about 20 different types of bacon at any given time. We tried to stock enough of each type to be able to fulfill between 5–8 orders of any product at any moment. And to make the bacon last as long as possible, we wanted to keep it refrigerated. With an average order of around four pounds of bacon, that meant we always had to keep close to 600 pounds of bacon on hand.

In the early days, this was out of Scott's house: yes—a house with 600 pounds of bacon in it.

Fortunately, Scott had a two-car garage and was able to convince his wife that they didn't need to put both cars in there. So we had the space, we just needed refrigeration. Where do you go for cheap refrigerators? Easy. Craigslist.

Tips for getting refrigerators off Craigslist:

- Free refrigerators are never a good thing—most likely they'll be power-hungry, old, and, for the most part, already broken.

- Don't underestimate the value of frost-free when it comes to a freezer.

- If "Free Delivery" is included in the ad, it means "if you come see this piece of shit, you won't buy it."

That said, in no time flat we had three refrigerators and one freezer running in the garage right next to our ship, label, and manifest station, which consisted of everything we needed to get the bacon from the fridge to the customers.

POSTAGE: GETTING IT DELIVERED

Four days before we were supposed to launch the site, we still didn't have an answer for actually printing the shipping labels. Scott had a "hack" of a solution that involved painful cut-and-pasting via the USPS website. It would work, but it wouldn't scale.

 Just Do It

NIKE SAID IT a long time ago, but it's as true now. Sometimes you need to just move forward. There was never a doubt in any of our minds that we could accomplish everything we needed to do by the time we were going to launch. Although we didn't have an answer to the shipping question, we knew we'd figure it out.

In the worst case, we knew we could hand-print the shipping information on boxes and take them to the post office to have them weighed and priced in person. That would have been a huge pain, but it would still get our orders shipped.

Had we focused on finding a solution before we started building the site—or even worse, tried to solve it ourselves with custom code—we never would have launched. The fact that we didn't have time or the means to build it meant we had to find an existing solution. Which we did. In the eleventh hour. But that's how these things work. Scott searched diligently for the simplest solution out there, and it ended up being even easier than we expected.

Something to keep in mind with this and any other problem that needs a solution is that you can almost always do it the hard way if you have to. With shipping, we wanted an easy solution, but we wouldn't let it delay launching, because we knew if we had to we would just do it the painfully slow and laborious way. We were fortunate that we found a solution before launch, but we could have survived if we hadn't.

For as easy as their flat-rate shipping service was, the USPS website had to be one of the most complicated things in the entire universe. Even worse was trying to hook to their developer tools to be able to print postage directly from your own applications. We looked at stamps.com and a few other custom solutions and finally, through a total fluke and some random Google searches, we found endicia.com.

Endicia makes a set of desktop software and developer APIs that basically take all the pain out of creating postage. Not only that, it was relatively inexpensive (service charge plus a little markup) and it created fantastic-looking postage complete with our logo. It even worked on Macs. We looked like a totally legitimate and professional online butcher shop.

The best part was that we could use USPS priority mail and it would be delivered just about anywhere in the Continental US in three days. That meant we could ship on Monday, Tuesday, and Wednesday and still get bacon from Portland, OR all the way to Portland, ME with almost no problems or delays. Most of our bacon was cured, but not all of it, meaning three-day shipping was crucial. In the year we ran the business, we never once had an order that couldn't be delivered in those three days. Say what you will about the USPS, but they know how to ship boxes. (We're convinced that adding the "Perishable" label on the box made it move that much quicker, but we have no proof of that whatsoever.)

SHIPPING IT OFF

So the bacon was packed, the shipping labels printed, the postage affixed, the boxes sealed. Now what? We had a bunch of orders going out on a daily basis and none of us wanted to wait in line at the post office. Here comes another bonus of the USPS: drop-off boxes.

With pre-printed postage there is a paper trail that reveals who is sending the package. This means the post office will let you drop off the boxes without standing in line. They have these great self-serve stations that you just drop the packages into, and off you go. They look like a giant aluminum monster with a steel mouth. You lower the handle, throw a few boxes in, and lift the handle. Clunk. The boxes fall to the bottom. (During the holiday season we filled up three of these in a row and pretty much pissed off everyone in the post office, on both sides of the counter.)

Scott lived close to a large post office (one hop to the regional station), so once a day Kami would good-naturedly load up her van with boxes filled with bacony goodness and drop it all off at the PO. Later on, when we had office space even closer to the regional hub, we scheduled next-day pickup from our mail carrier. He wasn't psyched about having to carry all of those boxes of bacon, but we kept him happy with a few extra packages for himself.

T-SHIRTS ARE REALLY EASY

One of the most popular items on our site were the T-shirts, which didn't surprise us. $20 worth of bacon is gone after one morning. However, a $20 T-shirt with free shipping is something you may have for years to come, and they also make great gifts. Plenty of people bought our shirts as gifts.

One of the best things about shirts, though, is how easy they are to ship. With those, we didn't have to worry about cold packs, Mylar envelopes, or getting the product to the customer without the package waiting on a post office shelf over the weekend.

Due to their uncomplicated nature, we offered free shipping on our shirts, which we feel played a big role in their high sales volume. The actual shirts went into a Tyvek envelope that is pretty much indestructible. It's also almost the exact color and feel of butcher paper. So with the simple addition of a packing slip and a nice big stamp of our logo, the shirts were ready for the mailman (our postal worker was actually male, so no, we're not being sexist).

What We Did Right/Wrong

IF WE WERE going to start over again, we probably wouldn't pick a food that requires refrigeration to ship. Talk about making it hard on yourself. That said, we learned quickly and found the path of least resistance to getting the bacon packed and shipped off.

We also knew we weren't the first people to sell food online, so we worked hard to try and find stories, links, and posts from people explaining their experiences and techniques. If we were trying to reinvent the wheel, then something was wrong.

And while shipping bacon isn't easy, it's also a big reason the market wasn't saturated with other people doing the same. If you're trying to sell a dry-goods commodity like cellphone cases online, you are going to face a long list of competitors. However, start a bacon-shipping business, and it's you and the crickets out there. So, because we weren't afraid of the risks and complexities, we were able to do very well in the bacon space. However, we learned what maybe everyone else already knew—refrigerated shipping is a pain in the ass.

Selling bacon online was still rather novel, but people selling bacon-related items had a big head start on us. However, most of it was silly novelty items most people wouldn't buy twice, or bacon-themed T-shirts that were actually pretty lame. We did find some decent stuff out there, and some of it was worth selling ourselves. We assumed that if we could generate enough traffic to our site and then partner like crazy, we could potentially drive sales for products we didn't even own.

Before we launched, we talked several times with the people at Bacon-Shirts.com. They were a local Portland couple who had been selling bacon-themed shirts online for a couple of years. Amy and her husband, Warren, designed and printed the shirts themselves, allowing for much higher margins.

They had three designs, and they were 100% focused on bacon T-shirts and aprons—no other products, and all original artwork.

We really liked two of their designs, and so we worked out a wholesale deal with them. They provided us shirts and aprons at a discounted rate, and we sold their products on our site, carrying their products with our own inventory. This worked out great for everybody; we got to expand our product offering, and Warren and Amy were able to increase their retail exposure. We also partnered with them from the beginning, allowing us to launch with a broader range of products while we were still figuring out our own designs.

 ## When In Doubt, Partner

THE KEY TO a good partnership was making sure that the folks we got the artwork from got a piece of the action. The going rate was 15% of the gross sale of the shirts and the artists got to keep the artwork rights. It allowed us to have a great stable of shirts, and the artists got paid when their designs sold without them lifting a finger, nor us buying the rights to the artwork ahead of time.

But if you're not careful, managing all these micro-payments can become a pain. So try and create thresholds for payments (such as a minimum of $50 per check) or agreements to pay every three months or some other designated interval. Never forget that you're partnering to help *alleviate* some of the work, not add more.

Obviously we wanted to have our own shirts as well. The margins on T-shirts are decent, but they're best when it's your own product and you're not paying licensing or product acquisition costs. Holly had plenty of experience designing T-shirts, so in addition to a black shirt with our logo on it, she designed a simple outline of our pig accompanied with the phrase "Bacon Tastes Good." Internally, it was nicknamed "Big Pig." I can't imagine a lot of women wanting to wear a shirt titled "Big Pig," so we kept that name to ourselves.

■ Shirt mockup of the Big Pig

Scott kept his eye out for anything bacon-related that could work as a shirt, or other people selling shirts that we thought would be a good complement to our offerings. Within a couple of months, we had deals for several other bits of artwork.

We were quick to make licensing agreements with different shirt- and bacon-designs, but we were slow to introduce new products to our site. We ended up with the rights to several designs we never used, which was just fine with us. If a design took off on another site and become popular, we had already secured the rights to print and sell that shirt design ourselves. But we also didn't want to offer too many designs at one time, and didn't want to have any products that weren't just awesome.

However, Scott did find a woman who was selling hand-screened, framed prints of a design entitled "Bacon is like a little hug from God." He immediately reached out to her asking if she had any plans to sell that design in T-shirt form. When she replied that she didn't, we worked out an exclusive deal for us to sell shirts screened with her artwork.

This turned out to be our best partnership, as we sold almost as many of this shirt as our Bac'n logo shirt.

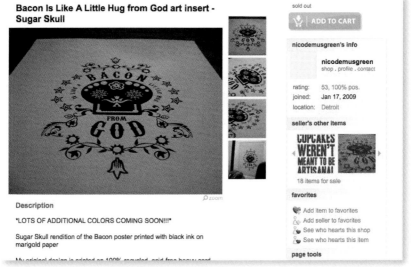

Bacon is like a little hug from God.

The toughest part about selling T-shirts is the different variations that are possible. You have women's shirts, men's shirts, and different sizes for each. And you have this for every single design you want to carry. Then there are people who ask for different colors of each design. It gets complicated, and the inventory can be tricky to manage. The easiest way we found was having dedicated shelves for each design, with clearly marked areas for each size. So in one simple glance, you could see every style of shirt in every size. If you were running out of anything specific, it was easy to recognize, allowing you to order more in time. You have to have quite a big set of shelves, though.

The best part about selling T-shirts was that they never went bad. They could sit on the shelf for months and it didn't matter. This is (obviously) why so many people go into the T-shirt-making business. For us, we hoped shirts would be a great addition to a bacon order, but the reality was most people bought either bacon or a T-shirt; they rarely bought both in the same order.

GETTING THE SHIRTS MADE

There's no shortage of people who can silk-screen T-shirts for you, locally or online. But finding someone good, quick, and affordable can be a challenge. Jason had a previous relationship from a project a few years ago, and so we decided to do our first shirts with the same company, Phantom Chicken in Portland, Oregon. He remembered them as being really cool, highly recommended, and doing a great job. Again, we stuck to our theme: *Find the easiest solution to start with. Adjust as necessary.*

Phantom Chicken is owned and operated by Greg and Gale Weiss out of their house/studio in NE Portland. And they are awesome. We may have gotten a slightly better deal if we had had our shirts printed online, but you often lose some of the customer service benefits when working with impersonal corporations. By working with people we already knew, and who specialized in small-batch runs, we got incredible service.

Before we had our shelving system in place, there were a few times when we didn't realize we were running short on a specific design until it was nearly too late. However, a quick call to Greg would result in his having more shirts ready for pickup in just a few days. Also, Greg and Gale allowed us to order shirts in a variety of sizes and colors without a minimum order for each, which is awesome and rare for companies who produce high-quality shirts such as those Phantom Chicken produces.

Other benefits of working consistently with a local shop were that they kept our screens on hand and we could order new shirts by merely picking up the phone. When you silk-screen a shirt, you're actually pushing ink through a screen onto the shirt, and the screens have to be custom prepared, which adds cost to the process. If you work with the same person and have a relationship with them, they'll usually keep your screens around so they can be reused when you need more shirts, keeping costs down as you go.

We would also pick up the shirts in person, and during that time we'd go over new printing ideas, ink styles, suggestions for ways to make the designs stand out, and so on. That sort of actual casual consultation helped make our shirts a great product of which we could be proud.

If you haven't had shirts printed before, it's a lot of fun to take an idea and turn it into a tangible item that you can wear. Clothing is often a conversation piece, and it's a big rush to put on a T-shirt for your own company. It's also not nearly as difficult as you'd think. Most printers will have very clear and simple instructions on preparing the artwork, and many will do all the hard work themselves.

With Phantom Chicken, Holly sent over the vector files and a guideline of the size we were looking for, and Greg made sure that the sizes were correct and that they'd get put into the right position. We also used a shirt mockup design that gave everyone a sense of how the shirts would look, and allowed us to play with colors and size of artwork before it was printed. (See the "Big Pig" image on page 71.)

 ## Finding a Good T-Shirt Vendor

PHANTOM CHICKEN WAS locally known for its work with bands and musicians (both local and national acts). When Jason was originally looking for a printer, there were a lot of people in the community who could vouch for Phantom Chicken's service, quality, and the fact that they were really great to work with. Obviously, when getting recommendations, try to find people who have worked with a vendor themselves. And don't cut corners on some cut-rate vendor. The flexibility, willingness to help us out in a pinch, and general consultation and experience we got from Phantom Chicken was far more valuable than saving a few pennies.

■ STICKING WITH SHIRTS

One of the decisions we made early on was what we *wouldn't* carry. Obviously, we were selling bacon, and we knew from day one that we would carry bacon shirts, but over the months leading up to our launch, dozens of niche and novelty bacon products started hitting the market.

Absolutely the most popular among all of the bacon-themed items was BaconSalt, with its growth and distribution becoming unbelievably huge. But there were also things like bacon band-aids, bacon mints, and bacon fridge magnets. Because the three of us were already known by our friends for our love of bacon, we had each gotten our fair share of these gifts.

They were fun, and we enjoyed their novelty, but they sort of made bacon a joke, which was what we were trying to avoid. So we made a firm and absolute policy: we would sell only bacon-related products that you would actually want. If the product's sole purpose was to make someone laugh, then we weren't going to sell it. Now, some may disagree with some of our judgments, but I really don't want bacon toothpaste or bacon mints. I want mint toothpaste and candy-flavored mints. I want my *bacon* bacon-flavored and that's about it.

In the end, our products became limited to bacon, t-shirts, and aprons (there was a deal with pillows at one point, and we shouldn't have done it, but it was a learning process and part of a bigger deal). We probably could have sold some of those novelty products, but gag gifts didn't really create the experience we wanted to exude.

The Pillow Fiasco

AS PART OF our affiliate deal with BaconToday.com, we decided to take on the sale of some of their existing inventory. While in theory this seemed like a good idea, in practice there was one not-so-great twist: the bacon pillow.

One of the founders of BaconToday.com, whose father used to be in the fashion industry, had come up with the idea for a bacon pillow. It was easy to make and required only the money for materials. Sounds great. However, it turned out to be more of a pain than it was worth. And we didn't know this at the time, but shipping pillows sucks. They are relatively light, but they need large boxes, which are a pain to pack, and then add to the shipping costs. Not only that, bacon pillows are a niche item: people aren't scouring the Internet for bacon pillows, and they weren't exactly buying them when they found them.

We agreed to buy up the existing inventory (about $500 worth) and then sell them on our site. When the deal was being made, the pillows seemed like a small issue and the larger affiliate deal was the focus, but it turned out that the pillows were a huge problem. Shipping them to Portland, OR from the LA area was prohibitively expensive and in the end, we just ate the $500 and didn't get the pillows.

And because we straight-out lost $500 on the pillows alone, the partnership never really worked out to our advantage. We learned two important lessons.

1. Be careful of "add-on" details to a partnership. Scrutinize those details even more thoroughly than the rest of the deal.

2. It's possible to use a partnership deal to get rid of merchandise you're not selling. BaconToday did it and it worked great for them, although not so great for us. But in a difference circumstance—say if they'd partnered with a site that was more appropriate for bacon pillows, such as one selling gag gifts—it could have been a win-win situation.

FINDING THE BACON

There are all kinds of bacon out there, most of it cheap and fatty and from who knows what kind of pigs. We wanted to sell only the best bacon, so we went on a search to find the best-of-the-best bacon out there. This meant lots of Internet searches and trying to find information about farms that sold great bacon but had little Internet presence.

KINDS OF BACON

In addition to the varied brands and qualities of bacon, there are many variations within bacon itself. You've got thick, thin, slab, jowl, back bacon, smoked, cured, nitrate-free, flavored, etc. You name it, there is a variation in size, cut, and flavoring that calls out to just about any palette out there.

As we mentioned earlier, we were going to be carrying close to 600 pounds of bacon at a time, which meant we had to be really picky about which bacon and variations that would include. Because of our inventory limitations, and the fact that bacon inventory is actually pretty expensive, we knew we weren't going to be a clearinghouse for bacon. We had to find bacon that was exotic enough that people couldn't get it in their local grocery stores, but not so exotic it would scare people off. None of us have actually tried jowl bacon, but honestly, it doesn't sound as appealing as thick-cut peppered bacon. We tried to imagine what would sell the best, while still being interesting.

SMALL SHOPS

When it came to sourcing the bacon, we found lots of small farms that cure and sell their own bacon. And the conversations with the farm owners were almost always the same. We'd find their website or hear about their bacon on some random website and then track them down. We'd call them directly, and the people who owned the farm would answer the phone. A 20-minute to two-hour conversation would ensue, covering any range of topics from the weather to politics to favorite ways to cook bacon, and then a deal would be struck. Much like the T-shirts, we worked out deals for wholesale pricing on much of our meat. It was actually pretty simple.

One of the most fun encounters was with Beeler's, a farm in Iowa. Beeler's makes a line of uncured, nitrate-free bacon in a variety of amazing flavors. Garlic Pepper and Apple Cinnamon topped the list for us, but it was matriarch Julie Beeler who took the cake. Scott had filled out a web form on their website and within five minutes got a call from Julie Beeler herself. She's a charming and funny woman who knows the bacon business inside and out. She loved what we were doing and we actually got to know her and her daughter fairly well as we discussed our plans, talked bacon, and even offered them some help with their own website. It was one of the strongest relationships we formed during our time with Bac'n.

■ Beeler's bacon, along with the perfect BLT supplies

Our other suppliers came from a variety of different places: Kentucky, upstate New York, Wisconsin, Arkansas, and right here in Oregon. The trickiest part was getting the bacon to us and then on to the customer. Some farms had a great product, but just couldn't ship it to us cost-effectively, and so, even though we wanted to carry their bacon and knew it would sell, we had to pass on carrying that product. Sometimes you have to turn down sales because the margins are so small, you're not even paying yourself for your time.

Other sources of bacon came through local meat distributors, the kind that also provide grocery stores with their inventory. We got our Beeler's bacon from Western Boxed Meat. However, after about ten months of working with them, we just weren't ordering enough volume to maintain a relationship with their sales rep, and we lost our supplier of Beeler's right before the holiday. This was definitely a bummer, and it was the only way we could get that bacon cost-effectively, so when that avenue dried up, so did our supply of Beeler's.

STORE-BOUGHT BACON

Fletcher's bacon is very popular in the Northwest, and is available at pretty much any decent grocery store here. It's not from the same small farms as much of our other bacon, but for a mass-produced bacon, it really is exceptional.

During our conversations with the folks at Fletcher's, we realized they didn't have national distribution or online ordering capabilities. But they regularly got requests from people familiar with their product and were now living outside of their distribution area, so Fletcher's quickly became very excited about the idea of us selling their products on our site, and thus to their out-of-market customers.

The same local meat distributor we were getting our Beeler's from also carried Fletcher's, and for a while, we were getting both brands from the same place. We had a few sampler packs of their different styles and flavors, and we moved quite a bit of their product. It was affordable, tasty, and a great complement to some of the other more exotic bacons we carried. It's always good to have a variety, especially when people were regularly asking for a recommendation on what to buy.

We probably shouldn't share this next piece of information, but after about two months of getting our Fletcher's from Western Boxed Meat, we realized that we could get the same bacon at our neighborhood Costco, and amazingly, Costco charged $3.50 less per pack. So we did what any savvy businessfolks would do; we bought our inventory wherever we could get it cheapest, which in this case was Costco.

SLAB BACON

A company out of Kentucky called Broadbent Hams sold awesome, unique bacon. They had a variety of different flavors and form factors, and one of our favorites was their slab bacon. Imagine a one- or five-pound slab of bacon. In the end, it's just unsliced bacon, but when you look at a huge five-pound chunk of pork, it's so visually arresting that we never saw anyone *not* physically or verbally respond to it. Usually with some variation on "Oh. My. God. That's awesome."

■ Five impressive pounds of bacon

It's like a choose-your-own-adventure for bacon. You get to slice it to your desired thickness. And besides that, it's very uncommon in pretty much any grocery store, so it was novel while not being a gimmick.

■ Our cohort Michael Richardson used his slab bacon to make "The Bacon Tube."

We took advantage of the unique form factor of this slab bacon and wrote several blog posts about it. We also showcased some fun meals you could make with it, such as Michael's famous Bacon Tube. The slab bacon was such an entertainer, we got several requests from people making sure their slab would be there by the weekend, usually because they were getting it special for a big BBQ they were having, and wanted to show it off to their guests. We even had some people beg us to overnight it when they realized our typical shipping wouldn't get it there in time. This proved the value of carrying unique inventory.

THE BACON FINDS US

Once we were up and running, we had several farms find us, usually hoping we would offer their bacon on our site. Mountain Products Smokehouse out of New York was a great example. They had these really unique bacon flavors, like chipotle, jalapeno-infused, and maple-cinnamon, that were just unstoppable from a flavor perspective. They shipped us a sampler pack and we fell in love.

The key to this was that we no longer had to be out looking for products to offer; suppliers were starting to find us. And once we had our T-shirts and bacon inventory covered, we were able to focus on improving the site.

 Resources

- US Postal Service: http://www.usps.com
- Sticker Giant: http://www.stickergiant.com
- Craigslist: http://craigslist.org
- Stamps.com: http://stamps.com
- Endicia: http://endicia.com
- Phantom Chicken: http://www.phantomchicken.com

chapter 5

LAUNCHING WITH A LIVE AUDIENCE

AS ALREADY MENTIONED, we were planning on launching the site at our first annual bacon party. Great idea, right? Lots of bacon fans would come; we would be the hosts; bacon would be the guest of honor … a perfect time to announce and launch our new bacon venture.

The problem was, throwing a party for nearly 100 people is a large undertaking. And we were trying to launch a website. And the date for both was only three weeks away. And there were only three of us. And none of us had ever thrown a party like this before.

This meant that there would be a lot to do right after we launched, because we weren't going to be able to take care of everything beforehand. It also meant we better get started on that party.

THE EPIC EVENT

When deciding what to call the event, we tapped our friends for help. We wanted it to be fun and light-hearted, but of course it also had to be rooted in bacon. Scott sent out a Twitter message asking his followers what we should call it. Within an hour or so, Kelly Guimont (@verso on Twitter) responded with "MasterBacon."

When it comes right down to it, the three of us are still little boys who giggle at penis jokes. So we laughed—out loud—and agreed it was a great name. It's not the classiest brand in the world, but it was perfect for the casual nature of the party. And seriously, MasterBacon? That's funny.

■ The Twitter message that named our event

■ LOCATION, LOCATION, LOCATION

The biggest problem in holding a bacon event was finding a location that would let us use their space. We didn't have a budget for renting a venue, and with our guest list growing by the day we knew were going to need somewhere fairly big. We were hoping to find a restaurant or lounge that would partner with us; however, many were sticklers about some law preventing other people from bringing food into a restaurant or uncooked pork and health codes or blah blah blah. Thus, the first handful of locations we called all declined our offer. Awesome.

But despite the first few places turning us down, or health laws working against us, we didn't lose heart. The economy was in the toilet and restaurants were hurting. We knew if we were patient, we'd find a place.

While we were hunting for a location, our vision for the event matured. It changed from the idea of a simple party where Scott would cook a bunch of bacon and bacony recipes and turned into more of an unconference or "camp." This type of event became popular with the inception of BarCamp in 2005, and seemed perfect with its inclusive, participatory nature. So we began shifting the focus from an invitation to *come* to an invitation to *participate*. We started asking everyone to bring bacon-themed recipes, which of course led to the idea of a competition.

Finally we got in touch with the Davis Street Tavern. It's an upscale restaurant in Northwest Portland, and the owners immediately understood the possibilities with our party. They not only agreed to let us host the event there, but right away started figuring out ways they could participate as well.

BarCamps

"**BARCAMP IS AN** international network of user-generated conferences (or unconferences). They are open, participatory workshop-events, whose content is provided by participants. The first BarCamps focused on early-stage web applications, and were related to open source technologies, social protocols, and open data formats. The format has also been used for a variety of other topics, including public transit, health care, and political organizing."—Wikipedia entry on BarCamp, taken June 6, 2010

The basic gist of a "Camp" is that anyone can come, they're almost always free, and everyone can participate who wants to. It's not just for invited speakers to lead discussions to a group of silent listeners in an audience. It's a collective effort of everyone who attends. It also happened to be our model.

After our MasterBacon event, the name we used for events became BaconCamp, and we partnered with some people in San Francisco to throw a BaconCamp down there. Eventually, several other BaconCamps emerged on their own, and we did our best to always send some free bacon and prizes whenever one was being held. It's a great example of the fun, community nature of both Camps and bacon.

■ The Bacone—the award-winning recipe from San Francisco's BaconCamp

As we worked with them, they made plans to have three bacon-themed cocktails for the event. The first drink was a bacon Bloody Mary called Porky's Revenge. The glass was rimmed with BaconSalt, then filled with bacon-infused vodka and Bloody Mary mix before finally being garnished with an olive and a small slice of thick bacon. It was amazing. They had two more equally relevant drinks: a Bacon Old Fashioned and one called the 7th Degree of Kevin Bacon. Their menu also featured pork-belly specials to round out the offering.

■ While pig parts are not a common beverage condiment, the Porky's Revenge with bacon was amazing. Don't worry, the green bean is just garnish—you don't have to eat *that*.

The Davis Street Tavern went above and beyond what we expected from them. They actually got excited, participated, and improved upon what we were doing. As we've learned, venue enthusiasm is critical to throwing a good event. If the best you can do is get a venue to allow you in their doors, your event won't be nearly as impressive as it will be if you find a place that will really partner with you and expand on your ideas.

THE BIG DAY

When the day of the event came, we welcomed 32 entries into the bacon-dish competition and nearly 100 attendees. We even saw a few guys with bacon tattoos at the event, and several people we had never met came in from out of town just to take part in a bacon party. Much like our personal research earlier, it proved that people *love* bacon. We even had a vegan there, willing to try some bacon "just this once."

■ Poached eggs on pork belly ... a chef's contribution

For the competition we had several local "internet" celebrities in to help judge the recipes. This was great, because many of them tweeted about the party and our sphere of influence grew to a much larger crowd than we could have drummed up on our own.

One thing the judges didn't count on was that after trying 32 different types of bacon dishes, they would be a little full, if not a bit woozy. Yet everyone powered through, and then washed it all down with drinks made with bacon. (We heard from a few later on that it took them a few weeks to want to have bacon again. So now we know that there is such a thing as bacon overload.)

■ Some of the tasty foods that people brought

At the end of the night we gave away a few awards to winners of differ-ent categories—bacon-themed prizes, of course. A few dozen pounds of bacon itself went home with the winners, along with some T-shirts and some bacon cooking supplies. It turned out to be a great way to promote and announce our launch.

Even though the event wasn't *about* our company, everyone noticed that we were launching something. And if there was anyone who didn't know about Bac'n at the beginning of the day, there was nobody at the end of it. We had great tweets about Bac'n, and the party and the launch were written up in the local newspaper. Not bad for an event that only cost us some sample merchandise and a few T-shirts (and a few years off of our lives).

■ GOING LIVE

On the day of the party, January 17th, we announced Bac'n, *and* made the Bac'n site live. It was an eleventh-hour effort to get everything in place, but the morning of MasterBacon we turned on the site and began accepting orders. Midway through the event, we actually got our first order. Admittedly, it was Scott's dad who ordered the first package, but still it was so good to know that everything was functioning correctly and the orders were being properly placed and tracked.

By the end of the following night, as we said goodbye to a weekend of MasterBacon and crossing our fingers that we hadn't forgotten anything major, we already had several orders. Plus, we were starting to get orders from outside the circle of our friends and family. The first order from a person we'd never met was a big milestone for us.

GETTING EYEBALLS AND PAYING FOR TRAFFIC

Obviously MasterBacon was not only a good time, but a chance to get some coverage for our launch. We were written up in the newspaper, and loads of tweets and blog posts were written about the event. Most of that coverage mentioned the new site, and those links were super valuable.

Even with the traffic coming from that media coverage, we knew we still had a long way to go. Most of the traffic would quickly die if we didn't continue to get other people talking about Bac'n. And we needed to get them talking about the site itself, not the party.

We sent emails and messages to most of the people we knew who had any sort of online presence and asked them to cover what we were doing. We talked about how we launched in three weeks, how our bacon was amazing, how the three of us were doing this as a side-project. In short, we talked about anything that could provide an angle, and anything that would result in blog posts, links, or general buzz.

When you're starting a brand new site, it's very hard to get organic traffic, because the search engines don't know anything about you. You have very few links pointing to you, and your site is new, and thus perceived as less trustworthy by Google. In the early stages, if you want real traffic you'll have to pay for it, either by doing something awesome, by buying advertisements, or both.

■ PAY-PER-CLICK

We set up a Google Adwords campaign with very specific keywords. You don't want to pay for terms as generic as "bacon," because with something that broad it's very hard to determine intent. Some people will search for bacon so they can find a photo of it, some will be looking for Kevin Bacon's most recent movie, others may just be seeing what comes up when you search for "bacon." The more specific your keywords are, the more you can tailor the results and imply intent. So we focused on things like "pepper bacon," "uncured bacon," "nitrate-free bacon," and used those ads to send people directly to the product area of the related bacons. When people are looking for a specific product, especially something as specific as "Fletcher's Pepper Bacon Slab Pack," the chance that they are looking specifically to buy goes *way* up. That's why we tried to use those keywords as often as possible.

 NOTE The more specific and detailed keywords are considered "long tail" keywords as an illustration of the normal distribution curve and how it has elongated along with the rise of the Internet. The term was coined by Chris Anderson in a 2005 *Wired* magazine article.

Google Adwords Basics

GOOGLE DESCRIBES ADWORDS as ads that "are displayed along with search results when someone searches Google using [certain] keywords. Ads appear under 'Sponsored links' in the side column of a search page, and may also appear in additional positions above the free search results."

Those ads are managed online at Google's Adwords site, and advertisers choose keywords and bid on them for their ads to be displayed when other users search for those keywords. Small text-based ads appear in the results, and each time they are clicked, the advertiser pays a small "per-click" amount to Google.

Google uses a bidding system, similar to an auction, to set the click prices for specific keywords, with more competitive terms being more expensive. It's a delicate art to balance your spending, your keywords, your ads, and your conversions to make sure you're making—not losing—money from the ads.

All major search engines have a similar offering, but at the moment, Google's dominance as the de facto search engine of choice kept us using mainly Adwords. It's a lot of work to manage your ads, and doing it over separate networks wasn't an option for us.

One of the great things about Adwords and other ad networks is that most of the time you can sign up and get started right away. The networks are open to anyone, and so long as your ads adhere to the simple rules, you can be getting search traffic in a matter of hours.

Keep in mind that Adwords and pay-per-click advertising are also the kinds of topics people write whole books on. To learn more, we recommend you start by reading through Google's tutorials and free information as a primer on the topic.

The problem with this approach, however, is that you might have a huge list of keywords with different ads. And managing all of the ads can be very cumbersome. You can put the keywords into large groups (so you're managing ads and keywords in a bundle), but then your keyword bids are averaged and may have you paying more per click on a specific keyword than you would if they were bundled in smaller groups.

Another issue is that as competition comes and goes, your own ads are affected. If a competitor creates new ads focusing on the same keywords as yours, your price either goes up, or your position falls. Pay-per-click ads are never a "set and forget" type of business.

NOTE Be careful when you get started with pay-per-click ads. It's easy to spend a lot of money really fast trying to get traffic, only to realize later that all your profits are lost getting people to order, and you're not making any money for your work.

But don't be afraid to experiment. We had decent results when we kept our daily limits low and kept a close eye on a small group of keywords. We focused on what set us apart, and what seemed to have the best traffic for the lowest cost. We then compared that to our site conversions, and went back and adjusted. We never spent a lot of money on ads, but it was a good way to spread the word early on, and we had acceptable results for our money.

We also tried some Facebook ads (which can be very cheap), but in our experience they didn't generate enough traffic. This was in 2009, so by the time you read this, Facebook may have changed . They have so much traffic that you should always give them a shot, but don't be afraid to pull the plug and focus on more effective methods if you're not seeing the results you need.

FILLING UP ON CONTENT

Another part of launching was adding content. In the process of getting and testing different bacon, we got plenty of photos and video of our food products, but we were still missing photos of our T-shirts. We also wanted to get some more content for our blogs. Content for blogs is important because it's a great way to improve search results for a variety of long-tail phrases, and it allows you to link to other people—which hopefully gets them to link back to you.

■ THE PHOTO SHOOT

On launch day we had only some simple photographs of our shirts. They showed shirts lying flat on a table—not the most stunning photos, but they showed the products reasonably well. We knew that photos of people wearing the shirts would be much better, though, and shortly after launch we scheduled a photo shoot.

We waited until we had all of our shirts in stock, in all styles and colors, and then we sent out an invite on Twitter to see if anyone would be willing to come and take part in the shoot.

While it would have been great to have a pro help us out, you do what you can with what you have, and that's what we did. We both had pretty nice cameras, and were reasonably adept at using them. Neither of us had formal training, but it's much easier to be a good photographer in the digital camera era with the freedom to take lots of pictures and get instant feedback. So we felt pretty confident in our ability to at least get the job done.

We didn't have a studio, but Jason was working out of a really nice office space owned by Laura Cary, of Cary Design Group. It was perfect; the office was large, open, and had gorgeous furniture and ridiculously high ceilings.

So we invited people to come out to the office for a casual evening. We promised endless pizza and PBR, as well as a few free shirts to those who showed up.

Scott brought in two large lights, the kind you see when people are working on a house outside at night. They were way too bright, so we pointed them at the walls and let them backfill in the areas we were shooting. Actually, bouncing the light around the room gave a warm richness to our shots that made the shirts look really nice.

Learn To Be a Photographer By Throwing Away Your Shots

ONE THING THAT we've heard from several photographers is that knowing what to throw away is just as important as knowing what photo to take. Take lots of photos, and throw almost everything out. Scott and I set out during this time to take lots of photos, and at the end, we had somewhere around 3,000 images just from this one shoot.

Obviously it took a long time to go through all of those photos, but we were merciless in our editing. Most image programs (including Aperture, Lightroom, Picasa, and iPhoto) let you mark or star an image. Then, you can rip through a large number of images quickly. It's easy to just flag images that are decent, and ignore all the crap that isn't. Then go through all the photos you just marked, and do it again, marking only the images that are great. Do this a few times, being more and more picky each time, and you'll find that 3000 images probably turns into a few dozen really great shots. When you're nearing the end of the process, then it's worth categorizing and labeling images based on content or perceived usage so they'll be easier to find later when you're looking for something specific.

The night of the shoot came and we ordered in a bunch of pizzas, plus had several bottles of wine and PBR. People came in slowly and we took plenty of time to meet and greet. We had a few drinks and some food, and we let everyone get comfortable in the space. After about 30 minutes, we started shooting and passing out shirts.

About 20 people showed up, both men and women, mostly in their mid-20s. We tried not to stage anything, but just asked people to be casual and hang out. Occasionally we'd get a few people together and take more formal photos, but many of our best images came from when they were just relaxed and we captured people just being themselves. People who are used to modeling look very comfortable when they know they're being photographed, but most other people still get a bit nervous. We addressed this by just taking so many photos while not asking them to pose specifically, they never really knew if they were being photographed or not, which led to more natural photographs. Oh, yeah—the alcohol helped too.

TIP It's a really good idea to have a shot list. Ahead of time, make a paper list of all the shots you need, and try to remember to refer to it, so that the next day, when everyone is gone, you don't realize you forgot to take a key shot you were counting on.

Our website had a large, horizontal banner on the homepage, and we were trying to take shots specifically for that space. In general, the aspect ratio of most DSLR cameras is 3:2, but for the banner we were looking for something closer to 5:2, so it would be hard to get a good shot without being very purposeful while taking the photo and planning ahead for the cropping that would need to take place.

Jason also had a second hopeful plan: to get a picture that would be interesting and usable for the homepage. He found an area of the room with a solid background, and set up the tripod. He then had each and every person come through, and took several shots of them, each from the same angle and the same distance away. He had them act goofy, do something fun, or just take a drink from their beverage.

Afterwards, he combined the best photos into a huge collage that appeared as if it were one very wide photograph of all of them together. By doing it this way, he had the opportunity to capture each person uniquely, in their best shot, and create a group shot that would have been impossible otherwise.

The collage took a while to build, but the results were awesome, and it was a great image for the homepage.

■ Some of the individual shots, and the final collage in the homepage

BAC'N BABE OF THE MONTH

Shortly after we did our photo shoot, one of the models, Kristin Reilly, posted some photos from the shoot online. A colleague of Kristin's from Texas, Belinda Strange, got in touch and said she'd be willing to do some photos in our shirts as well. She seemed to have some experience modeling and was willing to do it for free, so we mailed her a few shirts and she promised to send us photos right away.

Within about a week we got an email back from Belinda proposing that she be our first Bac'n Babe of the Month. We hadn't even thought of such a thing, but with the email came a few sample shots from her own photo shoot, and the results were pretty good. The quality of the shots was really nice, and it was clear that Belinda had modeled before. She looked great, and our shirts looked great on her.

We agreed, and Belinda became our first Bac'n Babe of the Month. We posted some photos on our blog, which of course got picked up on the Internet right away. Soon, we had several bacon-blogs linking to the photos, and we got a nice little spike in traffic.

None of us expected to be selling our bacon by selling sex, but the idea and the photos were delivered to us in such a way that we really couldn't say no. And all of the photos were classy; they just happened to highlight an attractive young lady wearing our fantastic Bac'n shirts.

■ Belinda Strange, our first Bac'n Babe of the Month

Within a few weeks of that blog post we had several other women emailing and asking if they could be the next BBotM. All we had to do each time was to send out a few shirts and some basic guidelines, and then, like magic, we got back great photos of attractive ladies in full Bac'n regalia.

TWITTER, SOCIAL MEDIA, AND THE OTHER BUZZWORDS

As we said, we tried a few Facebook ads and didn't see great results. It's possible we were doing something wrong, or didn't have the patience to use the system correctly. However, as we hope you've gleaned from what you've read already, ours was a constant balance of focusing on whatever provided the greatest return on investment.

▪ FACEBOOK PAGES

We did, however, have a Facebook page that we loaded with images from our photo shoot, some info about our company and products, and other things. We got some traffic to that page, but we weren't sure we saw a large conversion between Facebook fans and orders received, so we didn't spend too much time on it.

▪ TWITTER

We did get a great response from Twitter, however. We used our Twitter account quite a bit, to both announce random bacon information and to drive people to new content on our blog and our site. In this case, we had people following us who were active in their appreciation of bacon, and when we linked to our site within Twitter posts, it was common to get quite a bit of traffic as a result.

In order to grow our list of followers, and thus to grow our reach and audience, we would often do quick searches on Twitter for "bacon" and follow people who were writing about bacon in a positive way (while filtering for non-bacon fans, or mentions of other types of bacon). This gave us a decent following on our account. It's something that you can do anytime, only takes a minute every couple of days, and has big results.

We also constantly monitored Twitter for any mention of Bac'n. Because the word was used in the past with a different definition, we did have a lot of false-positives, but we also followed many people who were talking about us online and whom we hadn't met yet.

At one point we discussed automating our Twitter searches, and auto-following anyone who mentioned bacon or bacn in a tweet. A friend of ours built a script that could do this, and the script even checked to see if the person you just followed followed you back after three days. If they didn't, it unfollowed them in order to keep your ratio of followers to people you followed high. All of us wanted the results this would bring, but we also felt a little sleazy about it. In the end, we decided against it. You can decide for yourself if this is acceptable to your brand, but we wanted people to feel like we were giving to the Internet, not spamming it, so we stuck to white-hat practices.

Why We Hate the Term "social media"

WHEN YOU WORK in any kind of online capacity, you'll find lots of people claiming to be "social media experts." While it's hard to define the term "expert," in our experience the number of experts seems to far outweigh the number of actually successful social media campaigns. Thus, the three of us are always wary of anyone with the words *social media* in their title. It just seems to be a label for people who don't know what else to do with themselves, but who like playing on Facebook all day.

However, that doesn't mean that using tools and websites that are considered social media is a bad thing. And while none of us would ever claim Social Media Anything in our titles, we did use some of those tools to successfully extend our brand and drive traffic.

We mention this mainly to warn you about the buzzwords.

OUR BLOG

We already had experience blogging, so we stuck with what had worked in the past: covering the bacon universe. One of the categories of content we started was the Bacon Hall of Fame. Every once in a while someone would do something on the Internet with bacon that was just so awesome, so unbelievable, we felt it deserved more than just a blog post; it deserved induction into a hall of fame or something.

While it never really caught on, we dreamed that one day our Bacon Hall of Fame would be the "go to" place for everything awesome about bacon. We also knew that when someone did something really cool with bacon, others would be searching for it. And if we wrote about it, we had a decent chance to capture some of that traffic as people came to the web to find out more info on whatever it was that just happened. Of course, then the goal is to monetize that traffic with product sales.

▓ THE BACON EXPLOSION

One of the keys to this decision was the Bacon Explosion. In December 2008, right before we launched, a group of guys at BBQ Addicts decided to see what they could make with bacon on a barbeque. They wanted to do something mindblowing, and they wanted to do something that would get the world's attention. The Bacon Explosion was their masterpiece.

In short, it was a pile of bacon strips woven into a mat, covered completely by a thick, square patty of sausage, buried in BBQ sauce, BBQ rub, and topped with small pieces of cooked bacon. Then, the whole pile was rolled up into a tube and tossed on a grill for a few hours. The result was a gorgeous, crispy, log of pork that seemed to get everyone who saw it both repulsed by its gluttony and desperate to try it.

That simple act, well documented with photos and text, got BBQ Addicts millions of visitors to their site, coverage in mainstream media, a whole side-business selling ready-to-cook Bacon Explosion kits, and supposedly a book deal. We left a comment on the website—one comment out of hundreds—and with the link in our name we got thousands of visitors from their website to ours. That's how much traffic they were getting.

This also demonstrated the power of blogging. BBQ Addicts nailed it in terms of creating buzz around bacon. But journalism—i.e., chronicling other people's amazing feats—can be just as valuable, especially when other people are continually surprising you with what's possible.

BACN.ME

We also had that bacn.me domain, and midway through our three-weeks-to-launch cycle, we decided to use it as a URL shortener. At the time, tinyurl.com had become the grandfather of URL shorteners and had been surpassed by shorter domains with more features (like bit.ly). And with Twitter's 140-character limit, people were looking to shave characters wherever they could.

As dozens and hundreds of URL shorteners hit the market, we acquired the code for one from Bac'n friend Rick Turoczy. He donated the backend system that would allow us to not only offer a Bac'n-branded URL short-ener, but it had tools and tracking built in that allowed us to see which URLs were exploding traffic-wise, being spread the furthest, or had the most people creating unique short codes for it. And because our URL shortener was bacon-related, it got used for a lot of bacon-related content. This gave us a deep insight into what was popular with the bacon crowd, which we used to write more compelling blog posts.

Darin Richardson of Refresh Media did the design for bacn.me—as he had for bac'n.com—and so it was the perfect visual complement to our main site. We also used it to drive traffic to our products, as whenever someone came to the actual domain bacn.me, they were shown those fabulous pho-tos from our shoot of sexy people in our T-shirts.

■ The bacn.me URL shortener

EMAIL DELIVERS

A final piece of our marketing efforts was good-old-fashioned email. We had a simple signup on our site that allowed people to get on our email newsletter list. We were shocked when our list grew to over 100 people. But as it approached 1000, we started looking for ways to really put it to use.

It's boring and doesn't get a lot of media attention anymore, nor is it the buzzword of the minute, but we would send out email newsletters to our subscribers—people who *asked* us to send them stuff—and we'd include a coupon code for a small discount or announce a new product in our inventory. And with every issue, we saw a bump in sales. It's easy to forget about email marketing, or to use it only occasionally without a real strategy, but make sure you're capturing people who are willingly giving you their email address and asking you keep in touch. These people want to buy from you. All you have to do is collect.

Resources

- BarCamp Wikipedia page: http://en.wikipedia.org/wiki/BarCamp
- The Long Tail: http://en.wikipedia.org/wiki/Long_Tail
- Tinyurl: http://tinyurl.com
- Bit.ly: http://bit.ly
- Bacn.me: http://bacn.me
- Twitter: http://twitter.com
- Facebook: http://facebook.com
- Adwords: http://adwords.google.com
- The Bacon Explosion: www.bbqaddicts.com/blog/recipes/bacon-explosion
- Rick Turoczy: http://siliconflorist.com

chapter 6

MOVING ON INCREMENTALLY

BAC'N WAS STARTED on the premise that you launch fast and adjust as necessary. The only problem with that philosophy is that once you launch, you then have to do all that pesky iteration. Furthermore, the motivation to work is often driven by timelines: meaning, when you only have three weeks to launch a company there's no time for fear or second-guessing or avoiding difficult tasks. Once that impetus to work hard is gone (or softened), you can stumble right into the pitfalls of normal projects, such as laziness, uncertainty, and the desire to avoid the tedious, boring stuff.

In this chapter, we'll look at our attempts to take Bac'n from simply functioning to fully functioning, how and why we added a lot of content, and what we learned along the way.

WHERE TO START? SOMEWHERE EASY

It can be very daunting to wake up, look at your website, and ask yourself, "What should I do today?" There are so many things you want to change, so many things you're not sure how to fix, and quite a few things that you've only just now noticed need your attention.

One thing we tackled right away was moving from Tumblr to Wordpress (see Chapter 3). It was a good early project because it was a straightforward task that had clear requirements and objectives, yet would make a big difference right away.

Taking this "quiet" time to extend our design to the blog was actually kind of fun, too. It's one of those tasks that doesn't require making any difficult decisions, because the design and visual styles are already defined. It's almost like painting inside the lines. And after the whirlwind of launching, doing something simple and mindless was a welcome relief.

However, that doesn't mean it wasn't valuable. The reward was huge: an elegant destination for our posts. It also allowed us to cross-promote our products much better: we put photos of our T-shirts in the sidebars, and little ads for some of our more exotic bacons throughout the blog's layout.

CONNECTING OUR BLOG AND SITE WITH GOOGLE ANALYTICS

Moving to Wordpress had the additional benefit of allowing us to incorporate the same Google Analytics tracking code in our blog that we already had on the main site. This gave us the ability to track all of our visitors to all of our content, all in one place. As we've said earlier, we used the subdomain blog.bacn.com, and because the primary domain was the same, it was easy to combine our analytics, even though the blog and the main site were on two different servers running different software.

Google Analytics allowed us to track our conversions in a much more complete way. Rather than just knowing that someone bought a shirt after reading a blog post, we could now know that someone came to our blog from Google after searching for keyword "X," that he then went to blog post "Y," and there clicked on a link that took him to a product page where he made a purchase. That whole sales funnel was really interesting, and gave us insight into whether cross-promotions were or weren't working and how well they worked.

 ## Site Analytics

THERE ARE MANY different companies offering site analytics, but we've always used Google Analytics. In many ways, it is the industry leader and its feature set is very hard to beat. Also, like many of Google's products, it's free.

Some similar services we've heard good things about are Clicky, Mint, Woopra, and Piwik. Each offer different value propositions, but we chose Google Analytics because it integrated so well with our other services, such as Adwords.

Diving into analytics can be daunting at first, but it's fun to see just how many visitors came to your site and where they originated. If they came from search, which keywords were they searching for? As you dive deeper, and start tracking conversions and how actions you've taken on your site affected sales, it becomes not only more serious, but more interesting. You can use these hard numbers to draw some very real conclusions about how one change on the sales page increased conversions, thus making you more money.

As with search engine optimization, analytics is a broad and deep category we are only scratching the surface of.

In addition to conversions, you'll also definitely want to set up Google Analytics to track your e-commerce purchases. And by connecting your Google Adwords account to Google Analytics, you can get a clear picture of the value of your traffic, how different sources change that value, and what the costs associated with that traffic are.

Keep in mind that with Adwords, every person you bring to your site costs money. After we had built up a good sample size (100 orders or more), we were able to look at our average order conversion, multiply by our average order amount, and learn the monetary value of one visitor to our site. Obviously, not all visitors have the same value as customers—some buy, some buy a lot, some just look around—but with analytics we could start to gauge and guesstimate which visitors from which sources were worth the most. Then, when we were calculating our Adwords budgets and our spending per click, we knew if we were breaking even or edging into profitability.

By looking through our analytics, we found that our blog brought in a good portion of our early traffic. We knew that some of that traffic fed into our product pages, which then led to purchases. We could look at which blog posts were the most financially rewarding, and could write more posts like that. This was important because we didn't have to guess where our time would be best spent. Or at least, not guess as much; we now had a lot more information than just raw visitors.

It's easy to get blinded by traffic numbers. Thinking that more traffic is the best thing for you isn't always true. Where your traffic is from, what their intent is in visiting your site, and whether or not you can convert them is far more important than just eyeballs. If you get thousands of people coming to your blog because you post a ridiculous article about someone cooking bacon on a hotel room iron, but they don't buy anything, it's far less valuable than ten people coming to your blog after finding an article on nitrate-free bacon and three of them buying something right away.

Cooking Bacon on a Hotel Room Iron

During DjangoCon (a conference for developers coding in Django), our office hosted a Django code sprint. Several awesome people were in attendance, and a few of them talked us into giving them some free bacon. However, since they were from out of town, they got back to their hotel rooms with a package of bacon and no way to cook it. They may have had a few cocktails that evening, which may have made their thinking extra clear. Whether from the cocktails or just from those good strong developer brains of theirs, that thinking led them down a path that ended in them using the hotel room iron as a makeshift griddle and cooking their bacon right in their room.

Now, we won't name names, or even mention which hotel chain it was, but I'm pretty sure it worked as intended, although it may have decommissioned the iron from future use. We recommend just heading to your local Denny's if you really need a late-night snack of bacon. It's a lot easier, cleaner, and you're less likely to get a surprise bill on your credit card for a new iron.

It can be hard to know what's working early on. When all of your traffic is new, you're being introduced to people for the first time. You have no ongoing relationship with them, they probably don't know anything about your store or product, and they may be hesitant to buy.

But as your site matures, and people bump into your content over and over, they become comfortable with the idea of giving you money. There's also more content as time goes on, which brings more and different types of people, giving you the chance to better measure different traffic sources and behavior.

PICTURES HELP SELL

Once the blog was up to speed, we started revisiting some pages that seemed a little haphazard. In the early days, our thinking was to focus on helping people find all the different types of bacon we sold. We wanted to create an elegant way to navigate our products. However, as a result, we undermined the importance of showing great photos of bacon and having our Add to Cart button in a prime, easy-to-find position.

Our early product pages had lots of cross-promotion. If you were looking at Beeler's Apple-Cinnamon bacon, we'd recommend you look at Beeler's other products or maybe a fun T-shirt while you were at it.

This is a great idea in some aspects, but we think it may have distracted some users as well. And because we put so much visual emphasis on showcasing the different products we had, we did a poor job of showcasing the product you were actually looking at.

■ The updated sales page

So we redesigned the layout of the product pages. We lowered the cross-promotional material, increased the image sizes, and placed a really big "BUY NOW" button right next to the product, while removing as much extraneous information as possible out of the top 500 pixels of the site.

Now when you came to the product page, you were greeted with a large image of the product, some simple information, and a big opportunity to add it to your cart. Additional information was below.

This made the whole page feel so much more balanced, easier to read, less stressful, and, we think, higher converting.

TRACK YOUR CHANGES PROPERLY

But we'll be honest. We didn't do a great job of writing down our pre- and post-adjustment numbers or the date the change was made, so we can't say exactly how much our conversions improved. It was significant enough for us to notice the volume going up, but we failed to log the changes.

This illustrates a very important point. We were so used to moving fast, and none of us had ever really been in charge of selling something online before, so we were a little lazy in some of our reporting. Because we didn't properly document when certain changes were made, and each of us made lots of small changes all the time, it made it hard to know which changes were hurting or helping.

We learned that keeping a journal of your site updates—noting when you did something and exactly what you did—is a great way to be able to look back later and see decisively how those changes affected your revenue. Google Analytics keeps track of your history for you, so you don't even have to write down your performance metrics ahead of time, just write down when you made a change and what changes you made. Google Analytics also makes it very easy to compare two timeframes, and therefore to compare changes (so you don't have a good excuse not to do it).

■ Comparing two months traffic and stats in Google Analytics

It's also really smart to do A/B testing—serving up two versions of a page to different people, most likely a product, sales, or landing page. You see which version of the page performs better. When you've collected enough information, you kill the under-performing page and keep the higher-performing one. Then you create a new test page to replace the one you killed, and start over. As you cycle through different pages, always discarding the page that performed the worst, you slowly and accurately refine your site to the highest-performing layouts, colors, and headlines possible.

A/B testing takes time and patience. You can't judge too quickly: you have to wait until the trend is absolutely clear to really know which page is better. Huge sites like Facebook may get enough feedback in a few minutes to know how people respond. For sites like ours, new and with modest traffic, it takes much, much longer to get a feel for what improvements work. But it's worth it.

Google provides a free tool called Website Optimizer. It allows you to schedule, create, and track A/B testing, as well as multivariate testing. It's well documented and a great resource for people without the programming ability to code the tests on their own.

Finally, when we had a specific special or sale going, we would create Adwords campaigns and ads specifically for that sale. Then we'd build a unique landing page on the website just for the people coming from those ads. We'd hide them from the site navigation so normal visitors would never run into them. This allowed us to create specific promotions and offers and test them and their layouts, without affecting the primary website where the majority of our traffic visited.

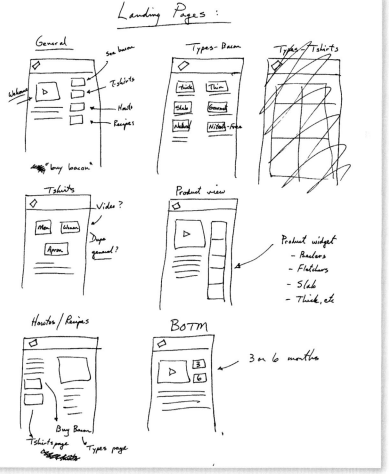

■ Here are some quick sketches outlining different landing pages for campaigns such as T-shirts, how-tos, and Bacn of the Month (BOTM). Notice how each one has a different layout, focusing on different content, but always pushing product?

■ INCREASING ORGANIC TRAFFIC

Google Adwords allows you to bring highly specific traffic to your site. Because you're choosing the keywords people are searching for, and writing the advertisements they will click on, you can be fairly confident about who is coming to your site and what their intent is. But Adwords costs money, and thus you have to be pretty careful to make sure your spending is paying off.

Free traffic, however, is harder to get. As stated in Chapter 2, other sites linking to yours helps build your trust within Google, and therefore raises your position in search engines, but how do you get other sites to link to you? And what about people who don't have a site from which to link?

Early in 2009, Twitter was just starting to go mainstream. Ashton Kutcher was the first person to hit one million followers, and Oprah sent out her first tweet. Non-techies were starting to sign up and come onto Twitter for the first time. And there was an explosion in using Twitter for marketing. All this time, we at Bac'n were watching closely what other people were doing.

One recurring theme we saw was giveaways and drawings. Companies would promise an iPod or whatever else was en vogue at the time, and ask people to tweet about the contest as their way of entry. People would tweet something such as "Enter to win an iPod from Startup X. Follow @twitteraccount, retweet, and win."

Even though companies were using it more and more, Twitter users didn't seem to tire of trying to win free stuff. So we at Bac'n gave it a shot ourselves. For four weeks we gave away a collection of different shirts or bacon packages, and had people do different things to enter each time. In general, we'd have them follow our Twitter account, or write a blog post about bacon (linking to our site), or tweet about the contest. Each week our audience grew as more people posted to their social networks about Bac'n.

It would be a stretch to call it wildly successful, but we got a few hundred more followers on Twitter, and about a dozen new inbound links to our site. These links were super valuable, especially early on when our site was still very new.

The biggest reward, however, came when Scott had the idea to invite our audience and fans to create their own special product sampler. We posted on the blog and our Twitter accounts an invite to create the best sampler imaginable, drawing from our existing product lineup. We had a few really great ideas, but the winning idea was in the form of an Economic Stimulus Package. This was during the recession (in case you didn't know that), and the creator used some creative explaining to show how our bacon would save you money. For instance, it included the Broadbent Hams Sun-Dried Tomato bacon, which allowed you to save money when making BLTs because you could make them without the tomato (we'd never actually recommend a BL minus the T, but it was funny nonetheless).

■ The Economic Stimulus Package

We loved it. It was unique and clever, got a lot of press, and was one of our best-selling products for a while. And the great thing was, all of it came from someone else, costing us only a version of the sampler she designed.

You have to be careful, though, with contests like this. When you're actively asking people to just create content and noise, some purists won't like it. We had one person, actually a friend of ours, call us out publicly for inviting our readers to actively spam Twitter on our behalf. Now, we didn't particularly agree with his point of view, but it is good to remember that not everyone is a fan of this type of aggressive marketing, and you need to know your audience.

> **NOTE**   To some people, tools like Twitter are for communication. When a company starts asking unpaid people to fill their Twitter stream with advertisements just to win a product, then other followers become subject to advertising in an arena they may feel is "above" that. Obviously, differing people will have differing views. But it's good to note how some people will react.

MORE CONTENT, MORE PRODUCTS

Part of improving the site every day was just continuing to add content. We blogged and we blogged and we twittered and we twittered. But we also wanted to find better products, either to continue to offer something new to our loyal customers, or to find something irresistible to our not-yet-customers.

The best way we knew to grow our product offerings was to continue to be on the lookout for new T-shirts or other bacon-themed content that stuck with our rule of not being a novelty. Unfortunately, not everything we wanted to sell, we could.

Someone recommended that we carry bacon from Lovelace Café, in Tennessee. We ordered some up to try and they were right, it blew our mind. The bacon came in some really interesting flavors, some of which sounded like a gimmick until you tried them, and then they were just legendary. The Hot and Spicy Jalapeno Bacon had little chunks of jalapeno layered in with the strips, and the cajun was so... cajun-y. It was all delicious. The problem was, we couldn't get the bacon at a price we could resell it for. And since Lovelace had their own online ordering, they weren't motivated to compete with us.

■ The gorgeous packaging was only eclipsed by the bacon inside.

We had the same problem with Nodine's. It was just fantastic bacon. They had one product, called the 10 clove garlic bacon (at least 10 cloves of garlic in every slab), that was unlike anything we had ever seen before. As you picked up the slices of bacon, instead of just some garlic salt, there were these perfect slices of garlic nestled right into the meat. We loved it as much as any other bacon we've ever had. Yet again, we couldn't get the numbers to work in a way that allowed us to carry the product and still make a profit.

■ Nodine's was some of the most unique and delicious bacon we've found.

We also tried to grow by making partnerships with other bacon sites. There were bacon blogs popping up all over, and most of them had no direct retail offering. There were a few that had some good business plans behind their sites, but where they didn't compete with ours, we tried our hardest to create partnerships.

In most cases, we worked out a direct affiliate deal with them. They would advertise our products on their site, and in return, Bac'n would pay them a small commission for every purchase made from their referrals.

There are lots of ways to track this, and there are companies who specialize in the management of affiliate marketing. However, unless your sales numbers are in the tens of thousands or more every month, it often makes sense to just do it yourself. We used Google Analytics goal tracking combined with referral and purchase metrics to figure out what sales were a result of which partners, and then we sent out checks every month.

Looking back, we should have created a minimum amount needed before people got a check. It's a pain in the ass to send someone a check for $4.65, and it's not worth anyone's time. A better way to do it would be to send checks whenever the affiliate balance reached, say, $50. Then you don't have to spend a ton of time every month making sure you're paying people what they deserve. Small things like this sound trivial, but they take up a lot of mind-space, and when you have a thousand other things to keep track of, those small issues are the ones that kill you.

This wasn't the worst mistake we made, though. One big misstep in our rush to partner with different companies came later. We happened upon a relatively new site that was getting a lot of traffic and doing a great job of blogging daily about bacon. And due to their commitment to blogging, and general SEO (search engine optimization) expertise, they were ranking very well for several bacon-related searches in Google. We wanted a piece of that traffic, and worked out a deal with them that included us selling a product of theirs on our site.

And get this: we actually pre-bought that product, so it was up to us to sell and recapture our out-of-pocket expense.

It wasn't our best business move, as we were basically giving them a sales commission on orders they sent us, with no commitment from them to do so. Plus, we had prepaid for their products, which we weren't sure if we could sell. Worse yet? The products didn't sell.

It didn't take long for us to realize we should have been wiser about our dealings. We've learned to be shrewder in negotiations and not take on liabilities that put us in a tough spot if someone else's products don't sell well. But, as they say, mistakes are opportunities to learn.

SXSW PARTY

The South by Southwest Interactive conference is arguably one of the biggest tech events of the year, if only in sheer volume. Dozens of companies throw elaborate and wildly expensive parties so that the tech elite will think their company is cool. Bac'n certainly didn't have an elaborate budget, nor were we even launching a new product, but we had to get involved somehow.

Scott started talking around and got connected to some people at Scene-Stealers—an online movie website with a smartass sense of humor—who were hosting three separate parties during SXSW, one of which was a bacon-flavored after-party, featuring the rude and crude rap group Bacon Shoe. We got involved, and we all started promoting this happy little bacon event during SXSW.

Bac'n brought several pounds of real bacon to the event, and we set up a small stand in the outdoor patio next to the street. Scott, Michael, and Jason all gathered around a griddle and cooked bacon to woo passersby. People would be walking down the street, smell the bacon, and before you knew it, were walking into our party. We of course would feed them, slap a Bac'n sticker on them, pass out some other merch, and shove them inside to listen to the band.

Bacon Shoe had a similar thing going, and while the two MCs rapped poetic on the stage, the DJ—dressed in a mangled dog/mascot suit—cooked bacon at the back of the stage. He even had a mic right down on the griddle, so through the music, you could hear bacon sizzling. When the bacon was finished, he would walk amid the audience like a waiter at a catered party, passing out fresh, hot bacon while the duo continued to perform onstage.

We'd never been fed bacon by a guy in a really bad dog outfit before. It was all very surreal.

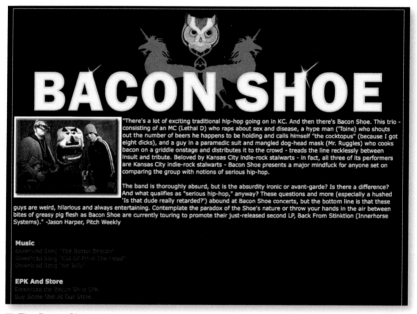

The band is thoroughly absurd, but is the absurdity ironic or avant-garde? Is there a difference? And what qualifies as "serious hip-hop," anyway? These questions and more (especially a hushed 'Is that dude really retarded?') abound at Bacon Shoe concerts, but the bottom line is that these guys are weird, hilarious and always entertaining. Contemplate the paradox of the Shoe's nature or throw your hands in the air between bites of greasy pig flesh as Bacon Shoe are currently touring to promote their just-released second LP, Back From Stinktion (Innerhorse Systems)." -Jason Harper, Pitch Weekly

■ The Bacon Shoe guys

To be honest, we have no idea if the party brought us many new customers. Things like this are very hard to track and measure, but it was a lot of fun. Most of our friends came by and ate some bacon, listened to some really random music, and had a good time.

At SXSW we also took advantage of BarCamp SXSW to host a session on starting a bacon company in three weeks. This may have been the most successful branding of all, as we had several hundred tech geeks salivating over our 20-minute talk about starting a bacon company using off-the-shelf software. We all made several great connections that day, and got to spread more of what was special about what we were doing.

■ THE RECOIL FROM SXSW

Upon returning from SXSW, Scott was promptly "let go" from his position at Vidoop. Yeah, he got fired. And when they explained why, he was basically told that Vidoop had sent him down to SXSW to promote Vidoop, but word was that he spent his time promoting Bac'n instead. We understood and you can't really argue with their viewpoint, we just happened to think Scott was capable of doing both …

Scott's position was pretty senior, so it's understandable that Vidoop was more upset over the issue of Scott than with Michael, who was also part of Bac'n *and* Vidoop and participating in our activities in SXSW. But Vidoop never said anything directly to Michael about it, and Michael never said anything back.

Hindsight being 20/20 and all that, it turned out that Vidoop went bankrupt and shut down entirely only a month or two after firing Scott. It wouldn't be hard to imagine that they were "upset" about the whole thing merely as an opportunity to not pay out the severance that would have been owed otherwise … or they just didn't like bacon. It's hard to say.

The lesson to take away from this is, if you're going to start a side project while still working full time, know how your boss is going to feel about it. And if that boss isn't into it, be careful how you spend your time on company trips. We'd all do the same thing again in a heartbeat, but Scott is living proof that off-hour interests can impact 9-to-5 jobs.

 Resources

Google Analytics: http://www.google.com/analytics
Clicky: http://getclicky.com
Mint: http://haveamint.com
Woopra: http://www.woopra.com
Piwik: http://piwik.org
Google Website Optimizer: www.google.com/websiteoptimizer
SXSW Interactive: http://sxsw.com/interactive

chapter 7

MAINTENANCE MODE & OTHER OPPORTUNITIES

DURING THE FIRST few months of running Bac'n, none of us really knew what to expect. We had been given some pretty optimistic numbers from Rocco at Bacon Freak before we started, so we believed in our ability to make money. However, as we moved past our second, third, and fourth month of business, we realized that our growth was definitely slower than we'd hoped.

We kept looking for small changes to make, and we tweaked content and design when we thought it would make a difference. But the little things failed to push us into the strong sales we were hoping for. After a while, some of the enthusiasm started to wear off.

Our AdWords campaigns brought people to our site and we could sculpt their experience based on the keywords they had searched for. We also used a coupon from Yahoo and got $100 worth of free search ads on their network. This gave more opportunities to test different approaches to our search traffic, try different keywords and ads, as well as just have a new source of searchers.

 ## Pay-Per-Click Coupons

GOOGLE, BING, AND Yahoo all desperately want your PPC business, and they're very aggressive in trying to get it. With very little sleuthing, you can easily find coupon codes that will give you $50-100 worth of free advertising on each of these networks when you sign up for a new account.

Some of those codes may require you to deposit a small amount into your account before the free credits become available, but even so, it's a great way to get free traffic to a new site.

And while it is most likely against the Terms and Conditions of the coupon, I have heard of people using different credit cards to sign up for multiple accounts—using different codes each time—to take advantage of the free credits. I'm sure this is frowned upon, and we'd never recommend such a dishonest practice. But it is possible.

 NOTE Each service may change these promotions, or terms, or ways in which they're enforced at any time.

But despite our best efforts, and the different approaches and different networks we tried, we could never seem to get pay-per-click to be profitable.

Terms as broad as "bacon" just weren't converting at a high enough percentage, even though competition for such an ambiguous keyword was low.

Terms like "Fletcher's peppered bacon" were much higher converting, but their cost was significantly higher, and with that expense, our margins were lowered to the point where we were barely making money.

■ Between Bacn.com and Scott's Flickr page, we had the top four results for the search "Fletcher's peppered bacon." At the time of this search, there was only one person advertising for that phrase—often an indication of keywords that are highly specific, have low competition, and low search volume (or, the long tail).

None of us wanted to be busy just for the sake of being busy. We wanted to be making money when we worked. So we weren't really interested in paying for traffic just to send orders without turning a profit. And because we had a hard time nailing down the right combination of keywords, ads, and landing pages, we decided to just shut down our paid search efforts.

Some business plans are such that you can afford to break even on ads and orders so that you can extend your reach and introduce yourself to a larger audience. But because fulfilling orders was a time-intensive effort, and maintaining inventory, keeping it cold, and keeping the materials for shipping (heat shields, cold packs, stickers, etc.) were all expensive, we didn't have the luxury of just breaking even.

A BAC'N IPHONE APP?

In early 2009, pretty much every business in existence was considering an iPhone app. It was a huge hype opportunity, and the buzz surrounding all the new apps coming to market was constant. The problem was, most businesses had absolutely no need for an iPhone app, yet they were all asking if they should have one or not, and many were deciding they *needed* one, more out of ego than real necessity.

Part of the reason for the mania surrounding the apps were the stories in the news about the crazy amount of money people were making for ludicrous time-wasters like the fart apps. Rumor has it that at one point iFart (an app that made fart noises) made $40,000 in two days.

■ Just a small sampling of the ridiculous number of fart apps in the App Store

And due to the large volume of apps hitting the market, the developers who could make apps were doing everything they could to capture some of the booming industry. They were making themselves available for hire, or building out apps of their own and hoping for some iSuccess.

So around March, Bac'n was approached by a group of developers from back east that wanted to build an iPhone app about bacon, and they wondered if we wanted to partner with them. They were actively looking for cool projects they could work on in order to get their name out and to build their portfolio. For them, this was a chance to gain some notoriety and hopefully turn that into business. For us, we thought it might get us some links, some buzz of our own, and hopefully some sales.

We really didn't think we needed an app for anything, but if someone was offering to build it for almost nothing, why not?

It was a good business move from the perspective of the developers, as they knew how to do the work, but needed a project that would provide a little bit of the money needed to build it. It was also a chance for them to ride the bacon craze and maybe get noticed by some of the people looking to hire developers.

At the time, it wasn't uncommon to hear of fairly simple apps being built for sums in excess of $10,000–$20,000. Apps that might take only a week or two to program. Because those with the necessary coding skills and familiarity with Objective C (the primary language for developing iPhone apps) were in such high demand, the developers were charging a premium for their time.

The group that reached out to us said they could build us an app for $500—an astonishingly low amount.

In some ways, we handled everything from here on out poorly. Because Bac'n wasn't paying our bills yet, we were all still doing this on the side, and that meant that at times we would be very busy with other things and doing everything we could to just keep Bac'n moving forward.

We should have spent some time investigating these developers, seeing what else they had done, where their expertise was, and getting a feeling for their level of work. But because it was only $500 and we were so busy, we just agreed without even really doing any background.

Spoiler alert: This was a mistake.

Jason whipped up some basic wireframes for an app that would allow you to "cook" bacon in a virtual pan. Giving the iPhone a little bounce would flip the bacon up in the air and turn it over. You could adjust the heat to alter how the bacon cooked, and you were encouraged to pull the bacon off at just the right time to avoid burning it.

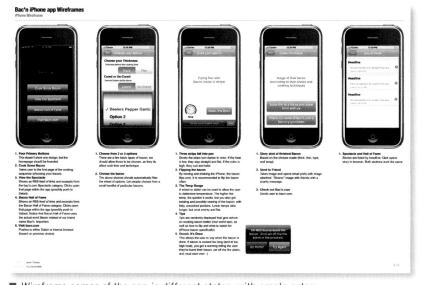

■ Wireframe comps of the app in different states, with ample notes

It was a simple app, but we built into it the ability to choose which bacon you wanted to cook. This was an opportunity for us to showcase and talk about the awesome bacon we had in stock, and hopefully get people thinking about the real thing.

The app would also have our Bacon Hall of Fame, as well as our blog content and some simple tips and tricks about cooking bacon in real life.

We planned on giving the app away and just using it as a way to promote our business. We didn't really care if the app made money; selling it for 99¢ and only getting 500 people to download it seemed shortsighted if you could give it away for free and get 50,000 people to download and play with your products, so our business plan was set. We just needed an awesome app.

The developers went into development mode, and time went by, and after a while, we all pretty much forgot about it. We'd paid the $500 and just kept working on all the things we had on our lists. Then, after a month or two, the first draft of the app arrived.

It was terrible.

The biggest problem was the graphics. It looked amateurish, and the interface was awkward and unresponsive. It was so far from awesome that we decided to not even bother making improvements, and definitely not to release it. We just shelved it.

It was a tough lesson. We wasted $500 and the time it took to plan and draw up the wireframes. We could have gotten a designer or illustrator to improve the visual aesthetics, but our budget wasn't really providing additional moneys for design and for subsequently retooling that design into the app. If we'd done our homework, or asked for design comps before production, we would have saved everyone some effort and money. Unfortunately, that was a lesson we learned too late.

■ A screen grab of the Bac'n iPhone app. Meh.

We'll never know if our app would have changed the mobile-bacon world, but in 2010, a similar app came out, offering the ability to cook bacon on your phone. It didn't see much traction, even though it was well designed. Perhaps the window for shallow, single-purposed apps dwindled after the initial gold rush of iPhone-dev-apps-mania.

A SIDE PROJECT TO OUR SIDE PROJECT

In May 2009, Vidoop continued to fall on hard times, and the team that Scott had worked with—Michael included—ended up being laid off. The team at Vidoop was great, but the market they were in was unique, and each deal took a long time to close. In the process of waiting for those deals to close, the company simply ran out of money. Several members of the team had become good friends and trusted colleagues, and Scott knew he would love to work with many of them again.

Bac'n was trudging along, and was still interesting, but the profit from it certainly didn't prevent any of us from looking at greener pastures.

Scott reached out to Michael, Steven Osborn, and Adam Lowry, all from Vidoop, to see what they could do together. Steven had been working on a few things in the mobile phone space and had some interesting ideas. He wasn't sure about the business potential, but the group started talking.

With Bac'n, Scott had learned a lot about building a business, and he wanted to apply what he'd learned to this potential new company and alliance. It was also apparent very quickly that the new venture presented a serious opportunity and that the market they were going after was going to be evolving quickly and drastically.

The group was uniquely poised to do something awesome. They were all available (a positive bonus of recently getting laid off), they were familiar with working with each other, and they had a significant level of expertise. Plus, the mobile space was changing drastically, which allowed newcomers the opportunity to be just as competitive as established companies. It also helped that they had a pretty solid idea.

The company was named Urban Airship, and they launched in June 2009. With this new venture, they took a few lessons from the world of Bac'n, which they applied right away:

- Have a business model from day one. For Bac'n, it was selling unique and high-quality bacon online to people who otherwise couldn't get it. For Urban Airship, it was providing for-pay infrastructure services for developers building applications for the iPhone.

- Launch in 30 days or less. Taking a page directly from the Bac'n playbook, Scott and Co. wanted to launch the company as quickly as possible, to see if there was a market there and to get ahead of the competitors that they learned had entered the space. Urban Airship formed on May 13, 2009 and announced at Apple's World Wide

Developer Conference on June 7, 2009—less than a month later. They landed their first two customers the very next day.

- Enter a space that is seeing lots of growth. While bacon as a meme was interesting, it was hard to gauge the actual size of the bacon market. Most of 2009 saw flat sales but picked up dramatically towards the holiday season. Urban Airship was in the hotly contested and rapidly growing smart-phone space. The big question wasn't "is mobile big?", it was "how big will mobile become?"

■ The Urban Airship website. Note, that's not a blimp, it's a rigid airship.

Scott was already stretched with Bac'n and other work he was doing, but the opportunity and team of Urban Airship proved too great to pass up. Around this same time we were moving into the new PIE space, and used the move as an opportunity to hire Akasha Becker to help with the day-to-day maintenance of Bac'n.

The Portland Incubator Experiment, Or PIE

AFTER A FEW months of working on Bac'n, the three of us started getting tired of weekend and evening work sessions whenever we wanted to work together. Scott was doing consulting and trying to piece together Urban Airship, Michael was taking on freelance work as a developer while also working on Urban Airship, and Jason had been working out of an office filled with designers doing Information Architecture on contract, and all of us were still plugging away at Bac'n.

As Urban Airship started looking like it could be a profitable company pretty quickly, and we wanted to be around other like-minded folks, we started searching for an office we could call our own. One where side-projects were the norm, and freelance or vendor work was just a means to an end.

We brought in a few other folks who wanted a similar space, and word eventually spread to Renny Gleeson, Global Interactive Director at Wieden+Kennedy, one of the largest, privately held ad agencies in the world. Renny asked what would happen if W+K provided a space for us, and we said we'd move in right away. They did and we did. And we've loved every minute of it.

Since then, PIE has become a collaboration with W+K, the Portland tech entrepreneurial scene, and a group of really smart, hard-working, startup-minded individuals. It also allowed Bac'n a home while the three of us took up workday residence together, working on all the random things we all do.

■ The PIE space. Big and open and geeky.

Akasha was a godsend. She was a friend of Jason's, and had some free time, so she came in and helped with all of those needy little details that come up when you're running a business and shipping inventory. She wasn't looking for full-time work, and we didn't have the money to pay her for that anyway, but investing in part-time help was worthwhile. We didn't want to screw anything up with Bac'n while we were busy with other projects.

■ Akasha the godsend, helping out at PIE, also modeling a Blazer's jersey, part of a giveaway for an additional PIE project.

As Urban Airship continued to take off, and Jason also continued to work on a second side-project, the three of us had less and less time to manage the day-to-day aspects of Bac'n. A few times, we ran out of inventory, or failed to get a shipment out on time. We hated to upset our customers, so we usually ended up covering whatever expense it took to make the situation right. Because of this, having Akasha around actually saved us money, as she was cheaper than paying to fix our mistakes.

But our appreciation of and dependence on Akasha also defined another problem: Bac'n was no longer our passion, and we had moved on.

PALEO PLAN—THE OTHER, OTHER SIDE PROJECT

As Scott and Michael worked on Urban Airship, I (Jason) started a second side-project of my own. Like Scott, I'd learned a tremendous amount starting Bac'n, and was pretty sure what I did and didn't want in my next project. I had also worked on a separate project the previous year, one that stalled and that I eventually left because of differences in opinion on how it should be run. Between that and Bac'n, I knew that from now on, I was primarily interested in simple ideas.

I identified that for the time being, I wanted a project that didn't involve a physical product: nothing that could spoil or that would be inventory on a shelf. That would mean I didn't have to worry about overhead or buying products before I could sell them. And I wanted a project where I wouldn't have to ship anything or buy postage.

I also knew I wanted a business that could go completely offline for two days without my customers getting angry. You start tying yourself to your computer when you work on a project by yourself or with a small staff, and people are relying upon your service. As you move away from providing physical goods, your service often moves to digital; and if access to that digital service is gone, your customers are easily annoyed.

I was committed to finding a business model that allowed the freedoms my previous two businesses didn't.

In the end, I founded Paleo Plan, a website dedicated to helping people follow a very strict diet known as The Paleo Diet. For a small monthly fee, the site provided a prescribed meal plan, recipes, and a shopping list for an entire week, every week. It was a tool of convenience to people, and it saved them 5–8 hours a week. Because of this, I could charge a nominal fee, get hundreds of people to sign up, and make a decent wage without having to manage the overhead of a Bac'n.

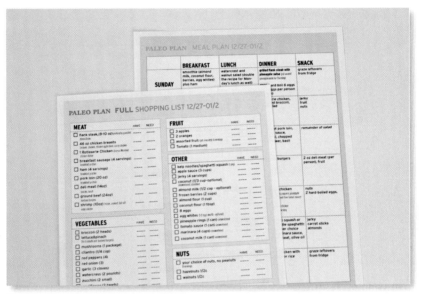

■ Paleo Plan's weekly resources

And like Bac'n and Urban Airship, I did it quick and agile. I launched in three weeks—started in the beginning of November and launched on Thanksgiving day. I used WordPress and other readily available tools and plugins to extend the site's functionality, and used a pre-made WordPress theme to launch, only going to a custom design *after* I had proven the business model and shown that it was worth more time and money.

■ Paleo Plan's version 2.0 website, which was soon updated to 3.0 in 2010

Bac'n taught all of us that you should invest the bare minimum until a sustaining business model was proven. And with Urban Airship and Paleo Plan, all of us found the revenue that we had struggled to gain with Bac'n.

HOLIDAY SHOPPING FOR BACON ONLINE

But we still had Bac'n, and after nine months of work it was slowly becoming less and less our focus. We all had moved on to other projects that were paying better and had larger potential. We all knew that Bac'n was a huge stepping-stone for us, but it wasn't the final destination.

And as we found other opportunities to pursue our interests, and our time became even more stretched, Bac'n started blowing up.

Apparently the holidays are a great time to give the gift of bacon, and we saw sales really start to increase. At one point during the holiday rush in early December we were shipping 400–600 lbs. of bacon a day! While this sounds great, it's a tremendous amount to manage. The mailman would drop off boxes for shipping along with boxes of bacon from our suppliers, and we'd separate it into the individual orders and then get it back to the local USPS hub to ship it out to our waiting customers, often in the same day.

The toughest part about this time of year was coordinating with the suppliers. While our demand for their products through bacn.com was soaring, they were also seeing the same demand through their normal retail channels, and making sure we had the right product when we needed to ship got tricky.

Worse still, having to deal with not having product on the shelf was really bad. Customers would order a variety of different bacons (one of this and two of that) and we would sometimes be missing one individual product to complete their orders. Much of the time we'd be missing a product because our inventory shipments were on backorder.

It was a customer-service nightmare. We wanted to get orders right, so we'd have to contact customers and see if they wanted a replacement, a smaller order, or to wait until our back orders came in. We also never knew when to pull a product from our online store, because most of the time we were hearing that our supply would be arriving "today or tomorrow," even when it took several days or weeks to arrive.

But the whole time, we knew that if we were going to do this, even if we had other things on our minds, we were going to provide the best service we could. We threw in T-shirts for late orders, extra bacon when a customer waited too long, or upgraded some of their purchases when we had more expensive bacon in stock (and they agreed to it ahead of time).

It was a tremendous amount to keep track of, and without Akasha, we would have failed even more dramatically. Had we been shipping those quantities all year, we would have created a better system. But because the orders previously had been so much smaller, we were ill-prepared for the quantity of orders and the administration it takes to fulfill them.

We definitely saw our "Bac'n of the Month" sales increase too, as bacon is of course perfect for gift-giving. We definitely could have gone even further, offering gift cards or promoting the idea of bacon gifts in our newsletter, blogs, and Twitter account. However, at a certain point, we were afraid of getting more orders because we were so busy with other things, and already unable to fulfill the orders we were getting.

It was an interesting problem, and one we didn't anticipate. And it paved the way for some even bigger changes immediately after the holidays.

chapter 8

SELLING BAC'N

DURING THE FIRST few months of Bac'n's life, whenever we talked about the business we were just as excited to discuss how we'd built the site as we were to talk about bacon. We understood that we were on the cusp of technology that would allow many more companies like this to happen, and we loved sharing our experiences. As a result of some of those conversations, in May 2009, we were invited to present at an interactive conference in Portland, called WebVisions. WebVisions covers all aspects of interactive, mobile, and "the web."

In many ways, that presentation formed much of the outline of this book. We discussed our early beginnings, how the idea came about, and then focused on the technologies and decisions we used to get up and running as quickly as possible.

It was a lot of fun, and the presentation seemed to really resonate with the audience. Out of all the conference sessions we've attended over the years, the ones that encourage people to take action for themselves, rather than teaching something their boss wants them to know, always seem to do well. (That, and we bribed the audience with a couple dozen bacon-covered maple doughnuts to make sure we held their attention.)

■ Somehow, bacon doughnuts just keep coming up. Here are some being served during Masterbacon.

But even during our presentation, we tried to use new, up-and-coming technology to allow for a display that wouldn't have been possible just two years prior. Throughout the talk, instead of text-driven PowerPoint slides, we simply had digital photos on a slideshow going on behind us. It allowed us to do the talk in a free-form manner, while stopping occasionally to give anecdotal backstory on certain fun images. The fact that it wasn't dry and predictable also kept the audience engaged.

The final thing we did was give all of the attendees a Twitter hashtag (#wvbacn) and asked them to post questions or comments throughout the presentation. With a handy yet discreet laptop, I kept an eye on a refreshing Twitter search for that phrase, and introduced audience questions into the talk as they came up.

We found this gave the audience the opportunity to shape what we talked about, without being disruptive. And when we mentioned certain things that they wanted more details about, they could ask for them easily without even raising their hands.

NOTE Clearly we weren't the first people to use Twitter at a conference, but we tried to use it in an innovative, non-distracting way that tied the back-channel to the talk itself, improving the experience for everyone.

Afterwards, during the small window when the audience can chat with the speakers before we're all rushed out and the new session begins, we were approached by Wendy Sharp, of Peachpit Press. She said she thought our story was interesting, and that others outside the conference could find value in our story as well. She wondered if we were interested in writing a book about Bac'n. It was a huge compliment, and we of course agreed immediately.

If you're reading this, it's obvious that the book deal was successful. But we mention this not to state the obvious, rather to point out that in the case of Bac'n, some of our success was completely unexpected. We didn't create the company to talk at conferences and write books, but the flailing economy created an atmosphere where do-it-yourself attitudes to business became very interesting to a lot more people overnight.

And while we made a nice profit selling bacon, the amount of social capital that we may have acquired by speaking at conferences, and now publishing a book, far outweighs even the most profitable of months of straight sales.

SIDE PROJECTS OF THE SIDE PROJECT DO BETTER THAN THE ORIGINAL SIDE PROJECT

Working on side projects is a gamble. You often don't know how they'll turn out, and when you start them, they're not your primary job, or focus. Depending on many factors they can become nothing more than a hobby, or they can become your full-time job as they become more and more successful. In our case, it was both, just not the way we originally expected.

■ URBAN AIRSHIP GAINS GROUND

Scott and Michael's new venture, Urban Airship, defined its service as "easy-to-use push notification services for iPhone applications." Basically, this meant that they offered a tool that allowed iPhone developers to quickly and easily include push notification functionality into their apps without having to build it themselves. When we were building Bac'n, we relied heavily on these same types of services, and now Michael and Scott were getting into the Software as a Service (SaaS) game themselves.

They also chose a great time to launch this particular product, as Apple had only recently allowed push notifications in their apps, and scores of developers were looking for an easy way to implement them.

In the fall of 2009, Urban Airship was gaining terrific market traction. They had sent over 30 million messages to over 5 million different iPhones. And thus, *their* phones were ringing off the hook. In late fall, they added a product facilitating in-app purchasing, and the momentum really started to build.

It was about then that they decided they were going to start looking for funding.

■ Continuing our tradition of food-based marketing, Urban Airship brought breakfast (alas, no bacon) to the hungry people waiting in line at Apple's WWDC.

There are many ways you can fund a company: using company revenue, getting bank loans, using credit cards, or raising external capital (which could be from friends and family, or traditional venture capitalists). Due to the business potential as well as the industry they were in, Urban Airship felt their only clear choice was to go after VC funding.

However, the process of actually getting VC money is such that you really can't have external distractions. You're constantly on the phone, flying to meet with venture firms, and putting together this or that presentation deck. As discussions continued, it became clear that Scott needed to divest himself of Bac'n to be able to focus 110% on the bigger opportunity of Urban Airship.

Bac'n itself was never a candidate for venture capital, and thus was probably always going to be a lifestyle company. It would be very unlikely for someone to acquire the company at the level of returns the investors would want to see, and its revenue would be unlikely to produce the profits either. So it made sense for Scott and Michael to focus on the larger potential of Urban Airship.

PALEO PLAN CONTINUES TO SUCCEED

Paleo Plan was also doing well, partially as a result of things we learned from Bac'n. I (Jason) knew that Paleo Plan could use help to gain even more traction and exposure, so I chose to use paid search; but I also knew that AdWords was a challenge to manage. So I approached Tom Hale, a colleague who had worked on paid search strategies in the past, and asked him if he'd be willing to manage my modest but growing needs for Paleo Plan.

This turned out to be incredibly wise.

AdWords made a massive and immediate impact on the traffic of Paleo Plan. Each one of the visitors from paid search was expensive, but the margins on the site were so large, it was possible to be fairly aggressive with the advertising budget.

For a young company, it's tempting to just do it all yourself as we had with Bac'n. But by having a professional not only manage the keywords, but build campaigns, advertisements, and make adjustments to optimize cost-efficiency, I saved enough money avoiding ill-performing ads that the cost of Tom's services were easily covered. AdWords is tricky business. Paying someone who knows what they're doing is sometimes the best way to save money.

FALLING FURTHER BEHIND

As Urban Airship and Paleo Plan continued to do well, it became harder and harder to keep up with the demands of Bac'n.

Each of us had trouble knowing exactly how to manage our time. Paleo Plan and Urban Airship were becoming far more profitable than Bac'n, and both seemed to have a larger future as well. However, we had invested a tremendous amount in Bac'n, and weren't willing to just turn it off because we were busy. But doing both meant we were doing neither very well. Orders went out late, and even with Akasha helping us we couldn't keep up with all of the small details that called for our attention.

There's also the issue with head space. Bac'n required only about an hour or two each day. That's not bad if it was contained. However, the mental energy needed to switch back and forth from one project to another, or to remember to spend that hour when Urban Airship or Paleo Plan had their fire alarms going off, made it much harder in practice. We weren't willing to say we *couldn't* do Bac'n, but we knew we weren't able to do Bac'n well.

INTEREST FROM A BUYER

Pretty much from the beginning of Bac'n, people would hear what we were doing and think to themselves, "Wow. I could do that! I really love *blank* and could totally sell that online." We had people approach us to buy our code so they could sell coffee, hot sauce, imported green tea, chocolate, fancy mushrooms ... anything where there are high margins on hard-to-find consumer goods of exceptional quality. The problem was, we didn't want to become a production agency making sites for other people.

We probably could have had a full business just helping other people make their version of Bac'n, but very few had any real money to put behind their idea, and we weren't interested in investing ourselves in everyone else's pet project.

Occasionally, though, we'd have someone mention they'd like to just buy Bac'n from us, and again, we usually dismissed them early on due to the lack of real money behind their offers. Even Rocco from baconfreak.com had shown some interest in the first few months, as we had built a competitor to his site using a totally different strategy, but his initial offer was way too low and came at a time when we were still trying to discover what potential Bac'n had.

However, in late 2009, with all of us getting busier, and our side projects eclipsing Bac'n, we started getting a bit more serious about selling the site. Scott and Jason put together a prospectus about the business, outlining assets, growth, traffic, the properties, etc. We shipped this around, and again got interest from Rocco.

■ SHOWING OUR NUMBERS

Before we could get a real offer from Rocco, we had to do some sharing of our internal sales numbers. In the prospectus, we used some vague generalities, but now we had to show all of our sales numbers for each month we'd been live. We shared our traffic numbers and sources, as well as the margins we were getting on our products. And while putting all this together was definitely a pain, since it was near the end of the year we would have needed to do it anyway for our taxes.

As talks continued, it became apparent that it would be much easier to do an asset sale of the business and not an outright sale of the company. This meant we could sell off the important parts like the brand name, creative assets, customer database, email lists, domain names, and inventory all in one fell swoop, and not have to do the legal wrangling of transferring the LLC from one party to another. There are other implications for doing this (namely, you have to spin down the original LLC afterwards), but it was a much simpler way to sell the company—especially since Rocco already had a business selling bacon.

The next phase was several days of back and forth, requests for some specific piece of information, and us finding it and sending it back. This is definitely the boring part of selling a company.

Eventually, we satisfied everything Rocco needed to see, and within a few days he came to us with his official offer (we're not allowed to discuss the numbers due to the terms of our sales agreement). We were excited to hear what the offer was, but that turned to disappointment when we saw it on paper. It wasn't insulting, but it wasn't enough for us to feel satisfied either. And thus, we respectfully declined.

CHRISTMAS WAS TOO GOOD

It was an interesting time. We were all very busy with our projects, and we had hoped to maybe make a nice sale of Bac'n and move on, but that didn't work. Scott was busy raising money for Urban Airship, and Jason was trying to keep up with a brand new business in an arena he'd never participated in before. Akasha was helping make sure Bac'n didn't fall apart, but we were paying her for her time directly out of our profits. And then, Christmas happened.

In any other business, going completely berserk during the holiday season is great news. Many online companies do enough volume during the gift-giving season that it can float several bad months to follow. But we were already stretched too thin, unprepared and just trying to not screw up, and with the massive influx of bacon orders, we were crippled.

Every day during December we had near-record orders. Secret Santas wanted bacon for their office-mates; girlfriends wanted shirts for their significant others, and holiday party planners wanted slabs of bacon for fun and interesting fare. We couldn't keep enough volume in stock, nor could we keep up with orders. We even ran out of our shipping materials, so we had to decide: buy a bunch more cold packs and heat shields, or figure out a better way to ship. We didn't really have a choice, and spent a grotesque amount of our profits on infrastructure.

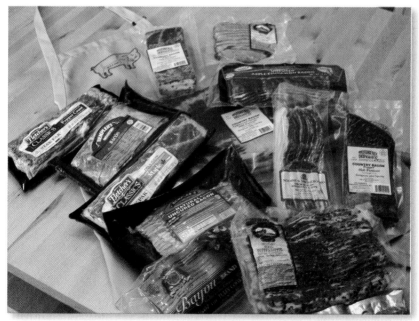

■ Our volume was terrific, and we were moving loads of bacon—almost too much.

ALL RIGHT, FINE, WE'LL SELL

During the holiday rush, we were also finalizing our book deal with our publisher. We'd signed the contract and were beginning to work on our table of contents, or more appropriately, the outline of the book. Not to get all meta on you, dear reader, but we realized that we were writing a book about our experience running Bac'n... to end the book with us shuttering our doors because we couldn't keep up with demand wasn't a very good final chapter. And we mean that both literally for the book, but also figuratively for our careers as well. Everyone likes a success story, even the modest success stories.

We recognized that if we sold the company we'd get some gratification from seeing Bac'n carry on, we wouldn't have to watch it crumble on bad press from missed orders, or come to resent it as it became a distraction. And, really, Rocco's offer wasn't terrible; we just had some pretty ambitious expectations. We also knew that if we kept eating bacon and stressing about everything, our clogged arteries were going to give us a communal heart attack.

■ Not even PBR could help solve this one.

So we gave Rocco a call and said we wanted to restart our earlier conversations. We made a counter to his offer, and he made a counter to ours, and we came to a nice middle ground, something all of us could be proud of. We'll be honest, though; we really loved the idea of ending our book—a book about starting a company in three weeks—with the story about us selling the company in under a year. It just seemed to have a satisfying, semi-symmetrical feeling of closure.

Once we agreed on a price, the sale was pretty easy to complete. We outlined the terms of the sale and what the agreement was, and had our lawyers look it over (about $250 each). Contracts were signed, and the paperwork side of the deal was finished.

▨ LOGISTICS OF THE SALE

The financial aspects are always the trickiest with any digital sale, so Rocco agreed to pay half the money up front and the other half upon completion of the sale (in this case, transfer of assets). It's a great way to negotiate, because while we totally trusted Rocco, it was nice for both of us to have something at stake from the beginning.

Delivering the assets and inventory went relatively quickly. Rocco agreed to cover all of the shipping costs for our inventory, which was a nice gesture (especially considering that the shipping invoice was pretty costly). Scott packaged up every pound of bacon, all of our packing materials, and a significant inventory of T-shirts and aprons. Then with one final trip to the post office, our Bac'n shelves became empty for the first time in over a year.

NOTE Keep in mind small things like the shipping costs of assets when negotiating the sale. They may seem trivial, but they can add up and it's good to know who is responsible for them. Also, when you accept a lower cost, you can often arrange these additional expenses to be handled by the buyer.

Once the hard goods were in the mail, we set about transferring accounts. We started with the domain name, then our phone numbers, all of our marketing accounts (such as Twitter), and other services like UserVoice and WordPress. This isn't hard, it's just time-consuming. We obviously wanted to change the passwords on each account, and then let Rocco set new passwords himself. We also forgot some things, and had to go back a few times and get the quiet little items it was easy to overlook.

Then we had to hand over the code. Because Rocco wasn't a programmer, and we had built the site using custom code, he was a bit concerned about being able to modify the site himself. We also didn't want to get into the game of doing that for him, even though the contract clearly outlined we weren't responsible for any modifications to the code, so we set out to find a programmer to help Rocco.

We wanted to see Bac'n succeed in the hands of its new owner, so we were motivated to help get Rocco going. We just didn't want to be doing development work for someone else's website. But within a few hours of asking around, Scott found a local developer happy to help Rocco, and the two signed a personal services agreement and were off and running.

And despite the fact that we wrote our own software, because Michael had used commonly established practices and thoroughly commented the code, from the first days working with Rocco the new developer had few questions. Michael didn't even have to go through anything with him as the site transitioned out of our care.

ONCE IT'S GONE, IT'S GONE

The sale finalized in January 2010, within weeks of our one-year anniversary. And like that, it was gone. It's funny how you can go from working on one thing pretty much every day for a year, then suddenly stop, and—if you're busy enough—barely even notice. Your mind just moves on to the next thing and you feel the warm, relaxing glow of the knowledge that you're not behind any more; that you have a little more freedom and a little less guilt/responsibility waiting for you.

In our busyness, the three of us went maybe a month or two without even checking back to see how Bac'n was coming along without us. Word had gotten out that we had sold the company, and we were happy to accept congratulations and warm regards from our friends. We celebrated the small victory of selling a company, and raised a glass in its honor.

Then, maybe mid-February, Jason pulled up the site to take a screen-grab for something. And he saw it.

Rocco had migrated the existing site into the platform that he used for Bacon Freak. Unfortunately, that platform was a bit homely. He also had adjusted many of the assets to fit in his existing system, but seemed not to have taken some of the time and care we had in preparation of those assets. The logos were pixelated and stretched some; images were poorly cropped. The background, our once elegant "ode to butcher paper," now looked more like sawdust. We were a bit shocked, and all very saddened.

■ The Two Bac'ns.

We realized that once something doesn't belong to you, you don't have the ability to protect it. And we also realized that a lot of people knew us for the Bac'n site, and they might not know that we had sold the company. While I don't mean to disparage the site now, we couldn't really tell people we had worked on it without a giant caveat. Again, it made us all a bit sad.

CLOSING DOWN THE LLC

The last step was to close down our portion of the shop that wasn't included in the sale. As we said, part of the due diligence meant rounding up every single scrap of paper that had anything to do with the company. If there is one shred of advice to take away from this book, it's this: keep everything that relates in any way to the business, preferably in paper form. Keep it all together in one place. Even if you shove it all in a shoebox, you'll be far better off for it later.

Scott was pretty good at that, but did have to spend a few lunch hours on calls with Bank of America trying to get this or that statement from eight months back.

When it's time to do your taxes and your books, you can waste a lot of time trying to do it yourself. We chose to find a reasonably priced bookkeeper in Portland to get all of our numbers in order. If you have the choice, always always always go with a bookkeeper. They do this for a living, they are familiar with the software, they have quicker ways of doing everything, and you don't spend hours hating your life. It's really a win-win.

Keep in mind that a bookkeeper won't be able to do your taxes; those you'll need to take to an accountant. But a good bookkeeper will be much cheaper than an accountant, and having all of your books together will save you plenty of money when you finally do have to go to your accountant. You ᵃn't afford not to get a bookkeeper, really!

ᵃce we did an asset sale of the business, we had to close out things like ᵃccounts and actually spin down the LLC. The bank accounts ᵃmake sure you get all of those statements from the account before you close it. Closing down the LLC involves a bit of paperwork with the state offices that handle that; every state is a little different, but for the most part, it's nothing to be afraid of. MyCorporation.com or LegalZoom.com are great sites for finding out what your state requires.

And with that, Bac'n LLC no longer existed. And the Bac'n we had built was, in effect, no longer around either.

 ## Resources

- Thomas Creek Concepts: http://www.thomascreekconcepts.com
- LegalZoom: http://legalzoom.com
- MyCorporation: http://mycorporation.com

chapter 9

WRAPPING UP BAC'N

WITH THE COMPANY sold, we've had some time to step back and let the experience sink in. Most of this book has been about our collective experiences or specific strategies we learned together. But now that it's over, our retrospective has become much more personal. So, with that said, please allow each of us to recap our year of Bac'n.

▓ SCOTT KVETON

There are a bunch of memories I'll take away from building Bac'n with Michael and Jason.

Jason blowing PBR all over me after laughing too hard. Michael responding to me so quickly when I'd say "we forgot about packing slips." Getting that first box of bacon from a supplier. Picking up the T-shirts that we'd designed and had made for ourselves. Getting a bunch of random people together via Twitter to dress up in our clothes for a photo shoot. Belinda. Packing box upon box of amazing bacon. Our mailman, who never complained about us loading him up with a boatload of bacon to carry on his route. The Bac'n banner. Jason being nervous about asking his wife to do the branding. Having random people on the street or at conferences come up to me and say "You're the bacon guy, right?" Sharing the story of Bac'n with anybody. Not doing anything too cheesy.

I'm addicted. I can't stop. Building something from scratch is just one of the most intoxicating professional endeavors you can take on, and doing one in a field that tastes good is just a plain bonus. I can't wait to work with Jason and Michael again, and I know that anything I start from now on won't be the last thing I ever do.

▓ MICHAEL RICHARDSON

It's been about six months since we sold the company. I'm finally starting to lose the weight I gained taste-testing all that bacon. Some things, like my belly, will (hopefully) go away. Luckily, an experience like Bac'n will stay with you forever. It changes everything.

I'll never forgive Scott and Jason for turning me into a bacon mogul. Not only did they forever ruin breakfast by pointing out how wonderful good bacon is, they opened my eyes to an entirely new way of thinking and implementing. I can't go back.

We learned simple but powerful lessons, and we continue to apply them every day. Iterate quickly, and don't let yourself get bogged down in details and distractions. You can't just sit idle and let things pass you by, and one of the best ways to do that is focus on the unimportant.

They also taught me the importance of having a strong team, and strong friends, at your back. I know that I can trust Scott and Jason with anything. Find people like them—your life will only be improved.

Building an empire based on cured meats is something that everybody should do at least once in their life. I understand that delicious salty meaty treats might not be your thing, but everybody has something. Going after your passion is something that you can, and should, do. Please go for it. You'll make the world a better place.

JASON GLASPEY

One of the biggest takeaways from starting Bac'n is that it's much easier than you think to just do something. You don't have to have permission, and you don't have to fear failure. The costs involved have also decreased enough that they're rarely the hurdle they used to be. In so many ways, the cliché of "the only way to fail is to not try" continues to ring true in my life.

As I've started side-projects and companies, some have "made it" and some have not. Some have garnered attention, and others silently slipped into the back pages of the Internet. But one thing that has been consistent is that every time I do build something, I become more experienced and more enthusiastic about the next project. And with that, I gain even more excitement and gratitude that online businesses have become my livelihood.

I still see Scott and Michael every day, and we continue to look forward to the time we all work together again. We also continue to encourage each other and celebrate both our failures and success stories, even when we're the only ones who know about them. It's been a blast working with them, and I'm lucky to have been invited into the team. Thanks guys.

If you've made it this far in the book, then congrats. Hopefully we inspired you in some way; maybe you even learned something. But, now, close the book and go boot up your laptop, it's time to get started.

INDEX

Google Analytics
    comparing timeframes, 111–112
    goal tracking, 118
    using to connect blog and website, 106–109
Google Checkout
    shopping cart, 47–48
    website, 58
Guimont, Kelly, 84

H

Heinemeier Hansson, David, 45
holidays, buying bacon as gifts for, 136–138
homepage, wireframe for, 56

I

iFart app, 126
images, including on product pages, 110–111
Intense Debate
    versus Echo, 50
    website, 58
iPhone apps
    for Bac'n, 126–129
    push notification services, 142

J

JS-Kit, 42
Just Do It, 66

K

keywords. *See also* Google Adwords
    effects of, 125
    "long tail," 93
    managing, 93
    setting click prices for, 92
King, Matt, 2, 7
Kveton, Scott, 5–6, 156

L

landing pages, sketching, 113
launch, timing, 17–18
launch party. *See also* bacon party
    day of, 88–90
    deciding on location for, 85, 87

holding at Davis Street Tavern, 85, 87
    planning, 84
LegalZoom website, 153
links, counting on search engines, 25
LLC (limited liability company), closing down, 152–153
logo design. *See also* brand
    capturing aesthetic in, 35
    deciding on, 39
    developing budget for, 31–32
    progress of, 38
    refining, 37–39
    reviewing, 33
    reviewing process of, 39–40
logo designers, being honest with, 36
logos, finding designers of, 30
The Long Tail website, 104
Lovelace Café, 116
Lowry, Adam, 130

M

Makin Bacon
    blog post, 44
    website, 58
maple bars, bacon-topped, 4
margin, considering, 19
market research, conducting, 12–15
MasterBacon event
    naming, 84
    success of, 90
media coverage, getting, 90–91
meme
    bacon as, 3
    defined, 2
minimum order, considering, 19
Mint website, 121
motivation, sustaining, 49
Mountain Products Smokehouse, 82
MyCorporation website, 153
Mylar envelopes, using, 61–62

N

name, choosing, 14, 22–26
Nodine's bacon, 117